WITHDRAWN

ONTARIO CITY LIBRARY
MAY -- 1999
ONTARIO, CA 91764

ONTARIO
LIBRARY

D0851950

ENCYCLOPEDIA OF MAMMALS

VOLUME 14
Ser–Tas

MARSHALL CAVENDISH
NEW YORK • LONDON • TORONTO • SYDNEY

SERVALS

The African small cats, genus *Felis*, belong to the mammal order Carnivora and the cat family, Felidae. Other members of the family include:

BOBCAT

LYNX

OCELOT

MOUNTAIN CAT

CHINESE DESERT CAT

MARBLED CAT

THE BIG CATS

M. C. Wilkes/Aquila

SMALL IS BEAUTIFUL

WHEN IT COMES TO AFRICAN CATS, THE AWESOME LION, CHEETAH, AND
LEOPARD TEND TO STEAL THE SHOW. BUT THESE BIG CATS RUB
SHOULDERS WITH SOME SMALLER YET EQUALLY FASCINATING COUSINS

The leggy, long-necked serval, often described as the cat world's version of the giraffe, is one of seven small cat species that inhabit Africa and parts of Asia. These cats tend to live in the shadow of their big cousins—the lion, tiger, and others—yet they display many of the same characteristics. Besides the serval, the other species discussed here are the caracal, the black-footed cat, the African wild- and golden cats, the sand cat, and the jungle cat.

The cats' ancestry dates back some 50 million years to a family known as the Miacidae. The cat family branched off around 40 million years ago, when the line divided into two main groups: the feliforms, comprising the cats, hyenas, and mongooses; and the caniforms, comprising the dogs, bears, raccoons, and weasels.

An early catlike animal was a form known as Dinictis. It lived in the Oligocene epoch (37–24 million years ago). Although its canine teeth were long

CLASSIFICATION

Cats belong to the order of carnivores, or flesh-eaters, that includes dogs, hyenas, bears, raccoons, weasels, seals, and sea lions. The cats are split into two main groups: the big cats (seven species) and small cats (thirty species).

ORDER

Carnivora
(carnivores)

FAMILY

Felidae
(cats)

SUBFAMILY

Felinae

GENUS

Felis

AFRICAN SPECIE

F. serval
(serval)

F. caracal
(caracal)

F. nigripes
(black-footed cat

F. aurata
(African golden cat)

F. lybica
(African wildcat

F. margarita
(sand cat)

F. chaus
(jungle cat)

and daggerlike, they were not as awesome as those of the legendary saber-toothed tigers that appeared from the Miocene epoch (24–11 million years ago) up to a couple of million years ago. The saber-tooths reigned supreme among the cats for many years. Cats recognizable as belonging to the genus *Felis* date from the late Miocene epoch in Eurasia, and from the ensuing epoch, the Pliocene, in South Africa.

Some modern researchers believe that the cats we know today evolved through three major lineages: Those of South America evolved first, followed by the small cats of Europe, Africa, and Asia, with the big cats and other medium-sized species such as the puma and lynx being the last to emerge.

Whatever its origins, the cat family is now one of the most widely dispersed of all animal families. Indigenous representatives are found on every continent of the world except for Australia and in most countries except for Madagascar and New Zealand.

The highly versatile jungle cat (above) *has one of the most widespread ranges of the small cats.*

Stephen C. Kaufmann/Bruce Coleman Ltd.

THE NAMING OF CATS

As ever, the cats discussed here get their names from widely differing sources. The sand cat, *Felis margarita*, gets its species name from a French explorer, General Margueritte, who was the first European to discover it when he led an expedition to the Sahara in the mid-19th century. The caracal is so called from a Turkish word, *karakal*, which means "black ears" and refers to the distinctive coloration on the backs of the ears. In parts of its range, the African golden cat is known as the "leopard's little brother" because it inhabits the same kind of country and is said to be extremely vicious when cornered. The black-footed cat's habit of sheltering in old termite mounds has earned it the Afrikaans name of *miershooptier*, which means "anthill tiger."

Although cats have proved themselves capable of adapting to very cold, mountainous regions, they are not found in the polar regions.

CAT CHARACTERISTICS

All cats, whether domestic or wild, are instantly recognizable as belonging to the same family, sharing obvious physical features, but there is great variety in size and appearance even among the seven cats discussed here. And across their range, they are found in diverse habitats, displaying individual adaptations to specific environments.

Nevertheless, all cats have a rounded head with a short muzzle; prominent, usually erect ears; large, forward-facing eyes; and long, conspicuous whiskers at either side of the muzzle. The body is generally sleek and lithe, the legs sinewy and powerful, and the feet relatively large and soft-padded. The five toes on the forefeet and the four on the hind feet all have sharp, hooked claws that are usually retracted; the only member of the cat family not to have fully retractile claws is the cheetah, a sprinting specialist of the African plains. It is thus the only one that leaves impressions of claws in its footprints. All cats walk on their toes.

The serval is a true cat of the grasslands, and it shares much of its range with the more robustly built caracal. The caracal is sometimes called the African lynx because of the long tufts of hair on its

The caracal's ears serve as "flags," helping the cat convey its mood to others.

ears—present also in the Canadian and European lynx. Unlike the caracal, however, the lynxes bear markings on their coats.

The black-footed cat is among the smallest of all cat species, yet it has a reputation for ferocity that belies its size. It is also known as the small spotted cat, and both of these names give clues to its appearance. This cat also has long, sharp canines for its size—another indication of its vicious nature.

The African wildcat looks like a large domestic tabby. In fact, its coloration varies according to its location. The African golden cat also varies in coat color and pattern, even between individuals. This cat is about as big as the caracal but is slightly stockier with shorter limbs and even larger paws.

The sand cat, or African desert cat, as its name suggests, is truly an inhabitant of the desert, and to this end has a thick, woolly coat that keeps it warm through the cold nights when it is active. The soles of its feet are covered with dense, long hairs; these protect the pads on the hot ground—although it rarely moves much in the day—and also help spread its weight on the soft, shifting sand to make movement much easier. It also has short legs, enabling it to crouch low to the ground as it ambushes its prey.

The jungle cat also has a name that gives a clue about its habitat: It is a denizen of wetlands and woodlands from Africa east across Asia. This cat has long legs, a short tail, a broad head, and short, dark, hairy tips to its triangular ears. ∎

(A)NCESTORS

All breeds of domestic cats are the result of man's selective breeding over the years, and all have descended from the African wildcat. This wildcat is similar in appearance to its European cousin but is generally less shy and nervous. Except for its long legs, it looks similar to a domestic tabby cat and sits in an identical way, in an upright posture with its forefeet placed neatly together. Today, the African wildcat is often found near villages and farms, where it interbreeds with domestic cats to produce fertile young.

The rarely seen African golden cat is sometimes considered to resemble the ancestor of modern cats, at a time when they moved from sheltered habitats into those that were more open. Many are found in those open habitats today.

Color Illustrations Dan Wright

THE SMALL CATS' FAMILY TREE

The thirty-seven species of cat are all closely related to one another. Most taxonomists place them in just four genera, with all the small cats being included in the genus Felis. However, some experts break down the small cats, placing the African golden cat and the caracal into the genus Profelis, the serval into the genus Leptailurus, and the remainder in the genus Felis along with various Old World small cats.

CARACAL
Felis caracal
(FEE-liss ka-ra-KALL)

OTHER SPECIES:
AFRICAN GOLDEN CAT
ASIAN GOLDEN CAT

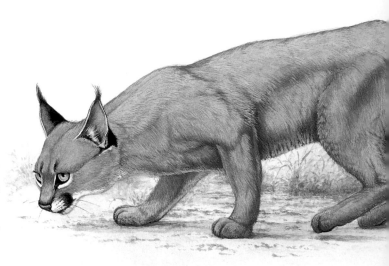

Occasionally classified with the lynx because of its ear tufts, the caracal is actually thought to be more closely related to the golden cats. A heavy species, the caracal roams the scrub, steppe, and woodlands of Africa and Asia. It can tackle and kill mammal prey larger than itself.

OTHER SPECIES:

PUMA
JAGUARUNDI
LYNX
OCELOT
GEOFFROY'S CAT
KODKOD
MARGAY
PAMPAS CAT
TIGER CAT
MOUNTAIN CAT

BOBCAT

SERVAL
Felis serval
(*FEE-liss SER-val*)

OTHER AFRICAN SPECIES:
BLACK-FOOTED CAT
AFRICAN WILDCAT
JUNGLE CAT
SAND CAT

The serval has the longest legs and neck proportionately of any cat. The legs are not an adaptation for greater speed, but they enable the serval to see over the top of the long grasses of the African savanna. This offers an interesting parallel with the maned wolf, a dog species that has evolved long legs to enable it to spot enemies and prey across the grasslands of Argentina.

AFRICAN
SMALL CATS

EUROPEAN AND
ASIAN SPECIES

EUROPEAN
WILDCAT

NEW WORLD
SMALL CATS

LION

SMALL
CATS

BIG
CATS

OTHER SPECIES:
TIGER
LEOPARD
JAGUAR
SNOW LEOPARD
CLOUDED LEOPARD
CHEETAH

B/W illustrations Ruth Grewcock. Lion by Peter David Scott/Wildlife Art Agency

ALL CATS

2009

ANATOMY: THE SERVAL

THE EARS

THE EARS

are very large, oval, and erect. The serval has especially good hearing because the ears work as "antennae" to pick up the slightest rustle of small animals in the grass. The backs of the ears are black with a striking white or yellowish patch.

The serval (above left) is the tallest of the African small cats, reaching 25.6 in (65 cm) at the shoulder. However, it is often lighter in build than the caracal. Both have a top weight of about 40 lb (18 kg), but the serval may weigh only 15.4 lb (7 kg). The smallest of these cats is the black–footed cat (above right), which has a shoulder height of about 10 in (25 cm) and a head-and-body length of 13.5–19.7 in (34–50 cm). It may weigh as little as 3.3 lb (1.5 kg).

PUGS

Pawprints, often referred to as pugs, are not always a secure guide to a cat's size. The tiny print of the black-footed cat reflects its small stature, but that of the serval is dwarfed by the caracal's print—although the serval is usually larger. This is because the serval is adapted to catching small rodents, while the caracal may tackle young deer.

BLACK-FOOTED CAT

EYES

All cats have superb vision. The maximum amount of light is reflected into each retina, giving good vision in low light. Cats can see at least six times better than humans in poor light. To protect the eyes in bright light, the iris contracts to a narrow slit. The eyes are positioned on the front of the head, giving good binocular vision for judging distances.

SERVAL

CARACAL

B/W illustrations Ruth Grewcock

SERVAL SKELETON

The serval's basic skeleton is similar to that of other cats. The highly flexible spine gives the cat extra speed when pursuing prey by increasing the length of its stride. It also accounts for why cats can twist in midair and land on their feet when jumping or falling.

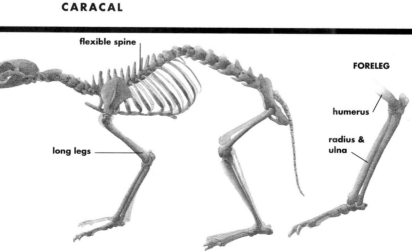

flexible spine

long legs

FORELEG

humerus

radius & ulna

SERVAL LEGS

In the foreleg, the humerus makes an acute angle at the elbow to improve leaping power. The radius and ulna are greatly elongated, giving the cat extra height and extending its stride. The hind legs bend sharply at the hock, increasing their leaping power.

hock

HIND LEG

X-ray illustrations Elisabeth Smith

CARACAL

The caracal's short coat is usually a rusty brown, with pale belly, inner flanks, and throat. There are no markings.

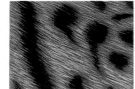

BLACK-FOOTED CAT

In addition to its distinct smoky-black paws, this species has a rich, tawny coat covered with black spots, bands, or rings.

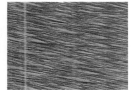

GOLDEN CAT

This coat can in fact be almost any color from gray to orange or even black, and it may bear any form of marking.

CLASSIFICATION

GENUS: *FELIS*
SPECIES: *SERVAL*

SIZE

HEAD–BODY LENGTH: 27.6–39.4 IN (70–100 CM)
HEIGHT TO SHOULDER: 21–25.6 IN (54–65 CM)
TAIL LENGTH: 9.5–17.7 IN (24–45 CM)
WEIGHT: 30–39.6 LB (13.6–18 KG)
WEIGHT AT BIRTH: 8–9 OZ (230–260 G)

COLORATION

BASIC COAT COLOR VARIES FROM PALE FAWN TO A REDDISH GOLD. FOUR BLACK LINES EXTEND FROM BEHIND NECK TO SHOULDERS. BACK AND CHEST COVERED IN BLACK SPOTS THAT MERGE INTO LINES OR BARS DOWN THE SIDES. LOWER AREA OF LEGS COVERED IN SMALL SPOTS UNDERSIDE PALER THAN THE PREDOMINANT COAT COLOR

FEATURES

VERY LARGE, ERECT, AND OVAL EARS; BACKS ARE BLACK WITH A STRIKING WHITE OR YELLOW SPOT IN THE MIDDLE
SLENDER, WHITE MUZZLE
VERY LONG LEGS; FORELEGS ARE SIGNIFICANTLY LONGER THAN THE HIND LEGS
SMALL FEET FOR ITS BODY SIZE
COMPARATIVELY SHORT TAIL WITH DARK RINGS AND A BLACK TIP
LONG AND SLENDER NECK

THE COAT

is always spotted and barred, but the markings vary among individuals. The base color varies from a pale tawny to a russet-gold; four black stripes run down over the shoulders; and the back, chest, and flanks are covered in spots. Generally, the markings are boldest in the driest parts of the range.

THE LEGS

are markedly longer, proportionally, than those of other cats. The serval's high profile gives it an advantage in the long grasses of the savanna.

THE TAIL

is fairly short, reaching only to the level of the hocks. Dark blotches at the base change to rings toward the bushy, black tip.

THE PAWS

are small and neat, reflecting the size of the serval's fairly small prey. The soles are naked. In common with all other cats except the cheetah, the hooked claws can be extended at will; they are normally retracted into the toes to protect the pin-sharp tips.

SKULL

Cats' skulls are shorter and more rounded than those of many other carnivores, but there is plenty of bone to support the large jaw muscles; these muscles achieve an immense biting force for inflicting fatal wounds. The jaws are hinged to give movement in one plane only; this restricts the ability to chew, but ensures effective use of the carnassials.

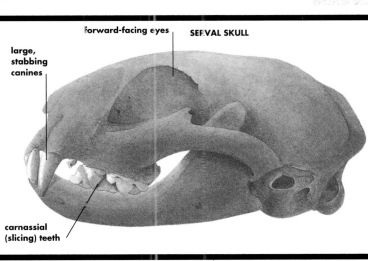

forward-facing eyes

SERVAL SKULL

large, stabbing canines

carnassial (slicing) teeth

BLACK-FOOTED CAT SKULL

The skull of this species and of the African wildcat resemble that of a domestic cat—small, neat, rounded, and equipped with typical feline teeth for meat shearing.

Color illustrations Steve Kingston

SHY COMMUNICATORS

OFTEN CONSIDERED TO BE AMONG THE MOST CAREFUL AND SOLITARY OF ALL ANIMALS, CATS HAVE NEVERTHELESS DEVELOPED HIGHLY SOPHISTICATED MEANS OF COMMUNICATING WITH EACH OTHER

Few cats interact much with others of their kind. The obvious exception is the lion, with its prides of up to thirty animals, but the small cats tend to be loners, meeting as adults only to mate.

In spite of their solitary nature, or perhaps more particularly to preserve it, cats have evolved various means of communication. They scent mark territories, for example, to warn off others but also to advertise their sexual condition. When cats do meet, they use a repertoire of sounds and postures that leave no doubt as to their feelings.

SIGN LANGUAGE

The African wildcat apparently uses at least nine facial expressions and sixteen different tail and body positions. These convey moods of relaxation, contentment, defense, anger, hostility, and readiness for flight or attack. The position of the ears and lips, as well as the tail, are used extensively to display emotion, which is why these areas are most often contrastingly colored or marked.

Wildcats are also noisy. Small cats use six calls, defined as hissing, spitting, growling, screaming, purring, and meowing. These are all means of "talking." Unlike big cats, small cats cannot roar— but by the same token, big cats cannot purr.

Cats probably developed much of their body language in order to reduce conflict with others of their kind. They are finely tuned to capture and kill prey quickly and efficiently; to this end they are armed with teeth and claws backed by powerful muscles. If they were regularly to attack one another, they would be prime contributors to their own destruction.

SUPER SENSES

All cats can be seen during the day, but their superb eyesight highlights the fact that they are active mainly at night. The serval, however, is more day-active than most, particularly toward the late afternoon. It will be very active for a few hours, then rest for a few more before resuming the hunt again. It may well hunt right through to ten o'clock in the morning or later. The caracal, too, may often be seen hunting during daylight hours.

M. Whittaker/Frank Lane Picture Agency

Rising from a nap, a golden cat scratches vigorously before setting out for the night's hunt (above).

Jonathan Scott/Planet Earth Pictures

NATURAL ANTENNAE

Cats are renowned for their excellent hearing, and none more than the serval. Indeed, this species relies almost entirely on its ears, since its principal victims are small rodents concealed in the tall grasses of the African savanna.

The serval has the largest external ear flaps of any cat. By straining them in the direction of the slightest sound—it can move them in various directions—it can use the ears as antennae. A cat's hearing range of 200Hz–100KHz extends well above that of a human's (20Hz–20KHz). The serval can therefore pick up the frequencies of rodent calls within the range of 20–50KHz—again, outside the register of human hearing. It can even detect the sound of rodents moving underground, and it will often wait by a hole in the ground for the hapless animal to emerge.

Small cats are generally more active than their larger relatives. This is because their prey items are usually smaller, so they need to catch and eat more of them. In addition to their night vision, they are aided by their sensitive whiskers. All cats possess these, the most tactile ones extending from the muzzle above the upper lip.

The whiskers extend beyond a cat's face, alerting the animal if there is a nearby object that it cannot clearly see. They also tell a cat whether it can squeeze through a gap or opening. And they are not just touch-sensitive: They can detect the least change in air pressure caused by a nearby object or moving animal. While a cat is resting, the whiskers project widely; when it closes in for the kill, they angle forward to direct the cat's bite. Furthermore, if the whiskers touch anything, the cat automatically blinks, protecting its eyes.

Unlike some of the American cats, the African small cats are not truly arboreal by nature. Most, however, can climb, and some may even take a kill up into a tree for safekeeping. Their claws help in this respect, giving them a grip on the bark on the way up. Once in the tree, they rely on their inherent balance to keep them stable. Cats that habitually climb trees tend to be the species with longer tails, which aid in balancing. ∎

Scratching helps to maintain the claws, but it also leaves a "calling card" for other cats in the area.

HABITATS

The fact that cats have colonized so many areas of the world is evidence that, as a group, they can cope with a remarkable variety of environmental conditions.

The serval is found across Africa, north and south of the Sahara, except for the most southern tip. It used to inhabit the Atlas Mountains of northern Africa, but it has not been seen in this region for the past twenty years or so. It is essentially a grassland cat, but it may venture into forest borders or open woodland, among marshy reed beds, and even in grassy mountain regions. It favors areas with a fairly high rainfall, and it also likes to be near streams or other water sources. It is intolerant of rain forest and arid, barren areas. Indeed, its spotted and barred markings give a clue to its favorite habitat. These patterns help break up its outline, concealing it better among the tall grasses. Superb predator it may be, but it has much to fear from its own enemies, such as leopards and hyenas.

The caracal occurs over much of the same area as the serval: It is absent from the Sahara, tropical rain forests, and parts of the extreme south. It also ranges across the Arabian peninsula into southern

African wildcats survey their range in the dusty, dry Kalahari of southern Africa (right).

Nigel J. Dennis/NHPA

Clem Haagner/Ardea

Asia, including Iran, Afghanistan, and India. Although more tolerant of arid conditions than the serval, it avoids the driest deserts, favoring instead semiarid countryside. It lives in brushland, savanna, semideserts, and dry steppes, as well as coastal forests and rocky uplands. Again, mainly a creature of the night, the caracal spends much of the day resting among rocky crevices or dense vegetation.

The black-footed cat is found only in the arid regions of Botswana, Namibia, and the Karoo, south of the Orange River. It favors the semiarid scrub veld, where the average rainfall is no more than 4–20 in (10–50 cm). It likes to have some vegetation cover—bushes or grassy clumps—and is rarely found in hilly regions. It is mainly nocturnal, passing the hot daytime hours in the abandoned burrows of a variety of animals, such as springhares, jackals, and foxes, or in old termite mounds.

The African wildcat is not fussy about habitat, its only requirement being a plentiful supply of rats and mice. The type of environment it chooses will

Long-legged and keen-eared, the serval is well equipped for hunting in the African grasslands.

DISTRIBUTION

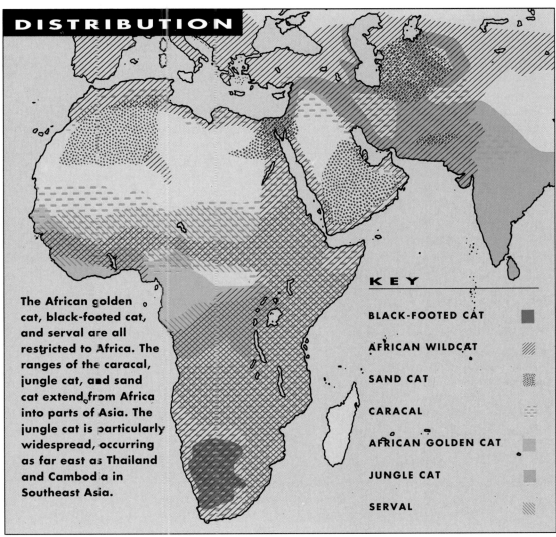

The African golden cat, black-footed cat, and serval are all restricted to Africa. The ranges of the caracal, jungle cat, and sand cat extend from Africa into parts of Asia. The jungle cat is particularly widespread, occurring as far east as Thailand and Cambodia in Southeast Asia.

KEY

BLACK-FOOTED CAT

AFRICAN WILDCAT

SAND CAT

CARACAL

AFRICAN GOLDEN CAT

JUNGLE CAT

SERVAL

(in)SIGHT

AFRICAN CATS IN ASIA

Many of the so-called African small cats extend into Asia as well. Two of them, the caracal and the African wildcat, although always considered as African species, are quite widespread in Asia. The caracal ranges from Saudi Arabia into Iran, Afghanistan, and northwest India and is as far ranging as any of these small cats. Africa's species of wildcat, the African wildcat, is found over much of the Middle East. Wildcats found around the Mediterranean—on Majorca, Crete, Sardinia, Sicily, and Corsica—are thought to be descended from the African wildcat rather than from the European wildcat. The diminutive sand cat is also found in desert areas of the Middle East and southwest Asia, extending into Russian Turkestan and Pakistan.

The jungle cat is found only in the extreme northeast of the African continent, in Egypt. The major part of its range is in the Middle East and Asia, but it extends deep into Southeast Asia. The island of Sri Lanka is another of its strongholds.

In the Asian parts of their ranges, these small cats may cross paths with the various Asian small cats. These include the marbled cat, Pallas's cat, rusty-spotted cat, and fishing cat.

affect its size; it also develops suitable coat color and markings to fit in best with the surroundings. Generally, those living in the drier areas have paler, shorter coats. The wildcat occurs across most of Africa except for western parts. It also extends into the Middle East, where it may cross paths with the European wildcat and the Indian desert cat.

Open or wooded country, mountains, and semidesert are all home to the wildcat. It is the cat species most likely to be found on village outskirts, where there are rats and mice. It has been seen, too, among the treeless, open grassland of the Ngorongoro Crater in Tanzania, where servals and caracals also live. In such open country, wildcats tend to take refuge from predators in holes and burrows dug by porcupines and bat-eared foxes.

The African golden cat has a relatively small distribution, found in central Africa from Senegal eastward to the forested regions of Kenya and northern Angola. It is primarily a forest-dweller, although it will be found on the fringes of some savannas. The wooded country it inhabits extends to altitudes of 12,000 ft (3,600 m) and generally comprises high rain forest or moist woodland. Although it can climb and will often rest on low branches, it mainly hunts on the ground. Its closest relative, the Asian golden cat, inhabits similar country—tropical rain forest and deciduous forest—in Southeast Asia.

The African golden cat's variation in coat color and markings seems to have less to do with its environment, for those with entirely different coloration may be found in the same area. However, those with spotted markings—both clear and indistinct—appear to occur only in West Africa.

The sand cat truly blends in with its environment, its pale coat matching the desert sand. It is found in the desert zones from Morocco and northern Niger to Russian Turkestan and Pakistan. Sand dunes are a favorite feature of its habitat, but it also skulks among flat, stony plains.

As a desert species, the sand cat is truly nocturnal. During the day, when temperatures may be well over 104°F (40°C), it is still and listless, in a state of semitorpor in which it seems almost oblivious to anything happening around it. It may shelter in a burrow, which it digs itself with its short, strong limbs; or it may just scrape a shallow dip in the sand. Lying here, it is practically invisible, but it occasionally falls victim to large, keen-eyed birds of prey. Venomous snakes have also been known to enter a sand cat's burrow and attack it.

Eric and David Hosking/Frank Lane Picture Agency

FOCUS ON

THE SAHARA

The Sahara in northern Africa is the largest desert in the world, covering about 3,320,000 sq miles (8,600,000 sq km) and including parts of eleven countries. This hostile domain is home to the sand cat.

Within the desert there are mountain ranges, rocky plateaus, boulder-strewn plains, and huge, sandy wastes, called ergs, where sand dunes can reach heights of 750 ft (230 m). Within the valleys, there are fertile oases where water is retained in wells or springs. These are the main areas of population in the Sahara, where people keep livestock and grow crops.

Temperatures in the Sahara range between extremes of blazing heat and bitter frost; in some parts, rain has not fallen for several years. Wildlife is understandably scarce in the most desolate regions, compared to many other deserts; huge areas are completely devoid of both fauna and flora. In other places there are plants that have adapted to the dry conditions, but many of these are very short-lived, completing a full life cycle in just six to eight weeks, their seeds lying dormant in the ground until the rain returns. Among the animals are gazelles, fennecs, gerbils, jerboas, and a variety of snakes and lizards. Barbary sheep live in the rocky plateaus and mountains.

TEMPERATURE AND RAINFALL

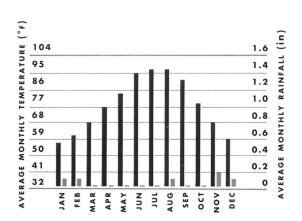

■ **TEMPERATURE**

■ **RAINFALL**

The Sahara is a vast cradle of intense heat and drought—it claims the world high-temperature record of 136°F (58°C)—but frost and ice are common in its more mountainous areas, and everywhere the temperature falls sharply at night.

The jungle cat extends only a little way into Africa. It ranges from Egypt and the Volga River delta eastward to Sinkiang and Southeast Asia, and also in Sri Lanka. It favors wetlands, woodland, or open country, from sea level up to elevations of 7,875 ft (2,400 m). By day it shelters among thick vegetation or takes over a burrow of another woodland animal, such as a badger or a fox. It also hides in the reeds along riverbanks. Although it usually hunts in the tall grass, it is capable of impressive bursts of speed—up to 20 mph (32 km/h). ■

NEIGHBORS

In spite of its hostile terrain, the Sahara is home to a surprising number of animals. All of these have had to develop special ways of coping with the extreme ranges in temperature.

EGYPTIAN JERBOA

Jerboas live in burrows in the sand. They emerge at night, hopping over the desert on long hind limbs.

SAND LIZARD

Many lizards make their home in the Sahara, retiring to shelters in the extremes of heat and cold.

Neighbor illustrations Craig Robson/Wildlife Art Agency

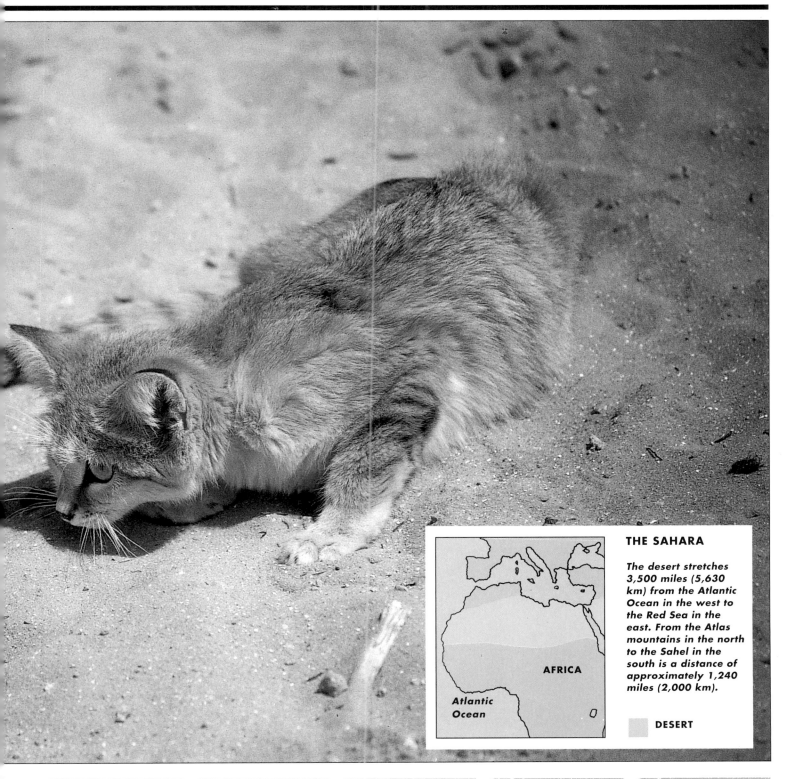

THE SAHARA

The desert stretches 3,500 miles (5,630 km) from the Atlantic Ocean in the west to the Red Sea in the east. From the Atlas mountains in the north to the Sahel in the south is a distance of approximately 1,240 miles (2,000 km).

AFRICA

Atlantic Ocean

DESERT

HARE

Inhabitants of Europe, hare species also range across Asia and south through most of Africa.

LOCUST

This tropical grasshopper breeds prolifically, feeding in vast swarms on crops and other vegetation.

LANNER FALCON

This African and Middle Eastern falcon is paler than its European counterpart, with a less marked crown.

SCORPION

Scorpions are related to spiders and live in warm, arid areas. They usually use their sting only in defense.

EGYPTIAN VULTURE

This bird can wield a stone in its beak to crack birds' eggs. Unlike most vultures, it has a feathered head.

HUNTING

Of all carnivores, cats as a group are the most consummate meat-eaters. While other carnivores, such as bears, include a large amount of vegetable matter in their diet, cats eat little else but animal flesh.

Most cats hunt and kill their prey in a similar way to one another. Although all are capable of short, sharp bursts of speed, they are not built to move really fast over a prolonged period. Even the cheetah, the supreme running cat, limits its high-speed chases to twenty to thirty seconds. Instead, cats need to be able to slow down rapidly so they can swerve after prey and to stop abruptly when they have seized it. Even the long legs of the serval are not designed to help it chase fleet-footed prey, but rather to increase its height.

IN PURSUIT OF PREY

Most cats prefer to ambush their prey or creep up stealthily on soft, cushioned paws. Often the final approach is taken at high speed; if the chase after a large animal is to succeed, the cat must bring down the victim either by tripping it up with an extended foreleg or by sinking the claws of its forefeet into the flesh and hanging on to topple the animal. In pursuit, the cat keeps its claws retracted. Not only would they soon become blunt if pounded over hard ground, but to dig them into the flesh of a flailing animal could bring equal injury to the cat.

Having caught its prey, a cat kills in one of two ways. Either it inserts a sharp canine between two backbones, severing the spinal cord and causing

Matthews and Purdy/Survival Anglia

almost instant death; or, in the case of large prey, the cat seizes the victim's throat in its jaws and suffocates it. Whereas large cats usually begin feasting by ripping into the belly, small cats tend to tear first at the thick flesh of the rump.

Most of the small cats discussed here depend for the major part of their sustenance on small prey, so a more usual method of attack is to pinpoint the

RODENT EXPERT

The African wildcat (below) is a natural at pouncing on small mammals, which often make up the mainstay of its diet.

JUNGLE FIGHTER

The jungle cat (below) usually hunts on the ground, taking rodents and birds, but it is quite able to tackle a fawn.

Like most cats, the serval catches small prey by pouncing with lethal speed and pinpoint accuracy.

location of the victim, then pounce on it. The serval is magnificent in this technique. It tracks rodents in the tall grass by listening intently, sitting motionless for up to ten minutes at a time. It is so sensitive to high-pitched sound that a high wind can confound its hunting completely. Once it has picked up the telltale rustle of its prey, the serval leaps high into the air and pounces on the victim. The cat pins the animal to the ground with its paws and claws. If the sheer impact of the strike does not kill the quarry immediately, a bite to its neck performs the coup de grâce. So accurately can a serval follow the movements of rodents in the grass that it is said to record a kill in about half of its pounces. Other cats are lucky if they do so in more than one of five attempts.

Sometimes the serval hunts by making a series of leaps across the grassland. This gives it a wider view of the immediate area, and also has the effect of startling and flushing out the small rodents. As they scurry away in alarm, the serval strikes with lightning speed and military accuracy.

Lacking the ability to grind their jaws laterally, cats cannot chew effectively, so they must pull the flesh off their victims in strips and swallow it whole. Usually, the comparatively small incisors at the front of the mouth are used to grip the prey and then to rip off any fur or feathers—these are discarded before the meat is consumed. The carnassials shear through the flesh, but only one upper and lower pair can be used at a time, which is why cats may be seen feeding with their heads to one side. The cat's rough tongue can be put to good use to strip large bones of the last scraps of flesh.

LIGHT MEALS

Most of the small cats feed on fairly small prey. A notable exception is the caracal. The fact that it lives in a wide variety of habitats means that it is a more opportunistic feeder than most of its relatives. Mammals make up the mainstay of its diet, and it regularly takes animals larger than itself. The fact that it quite frequently preys on sheep has made it unpopular with farmers; it will tackle a ram weighing 77 lb (35 kg) with no problem. It also kills goats and all manner of antelopes: springbok, steenboks, duikers, mountain reedbuck, and small kudu. It may consume large prey there and then or drag it to the nearest cover. Sometimes it rakes grass and other vegetation over a carcass to hide it for later consumption, but a fair percentage of the large antelopes killed are left to rot.

In some areas, rock hyraxes make up the bulk of the caracal's diet, and it will also kill and consume jackals, foxes, springhares, hares, rabbits, mongooses, and small rodents of all kinds. It has even been known to prey on the smaller African wildcat where their ranges overlap. The caracal will often take small prey items up into a tree to consume at leisure in the safety of the branches.

OPPORTUNIST
The caracal (right) will eat whatever it can catch, even to the extent of swatting birds out of the air.

Illustration Simon Turvey/Wildlife Art Agency

This extremely agile cat is also good at leaping into the air, so birds are often included in the diet. It catches them in dramatic fashion, by leaping completely off the ground and swiping at birds flying up from the ground. So accurate is the caracal's leap that it has been known to bring down two birds from a flock with just one leap. It also climbs trees to pounce on birds roosting in low branches.

The serval's diet consists of far smaller items—mainly small rodents such as grass rats and mole rats. It has developed a unique technique to capture mole rats. Locating a tunnel entrance in the grass, it digs into it, then sits silently by, one paw raised. As soon as the mole rat emerges, the serval hooks it with its claws, flings it to the ground, then pounces on it before it has a chance to scamper off.

Like the caracal, the serval will leap into the air to swipe at a low-flying bird—its long legs enable it to leap 10 ft (3 m) off the ground. It has also been seen hooking fish out of streams. Reptiles, frogs, lizards, and invertebrates make up any shortfall in the diet. Servals tend to wander farther afield than most cats in pursuit of prey, covering up to two-and-a-half miles (up to four kilometers) each night.

The diet of the African wildcat varies greatly with its location, but mainly comprises squirrels, hares, and springhares. It also eats insects, frogs, and reptiles, including snakes. These cats are apparently fond of birds; in areas near settlements they often raid poultry houses.

The black-footed cat feeds on small rodents, reptiles, insects, and spiders. It also takes ground-nesting birds when it can. Generally it hunts by

J. & D. Bartlett/Survival Anglia

An African wildcat in Etosha National Park, Namibia (above). *Like most cats, it is poorly suited to the high-speed chase, preferring to ambush.*

LONE MARAUDER

The solitary golden cat (below) usually hunts rodents and hyraxes. When it has to, it will tackle birds.

(in) S I G H T

SHARING THE LAND

The serval and caracal are of similar size and occupy much of the same savanna habitat. It may seem surprising, therefore, that they manage to thrive side by side.

The caracal is a bolder, more lively cat whose ability to adapt to varied habitats has made it a skilled, opportunistic feeder. Its powerful legs and larger paws enable it to kill animals that are far larger than itself, and just one of these may provide a meal for several days. It will also leave the grasslands to hunt in more open terrain.

The serval, on the other hand, is a true grassland specialist. All its adaptations—long legs, extrasensitive hearing, and smaller paws—make it the supreme hunter in this environment, and its diet consists almost solely of small grassland animals. These the caracal catches only occasionally to make up for any shortfall in its diet.

stealth and ambush, creeping silently from its shelter among a rocky outcrop or a burrow. However, its vicious nature comes to the fore when dealing with relatively large prey; then it will hurl itself at the victim, clutching and raking at it with its claws as it tries to deliver a fatal bite. So tightly does it cling to the hapless animal that often the two will roll over and over on the ground together.

The African golden cat slinks around villages and settlements to raid poultry houses and to prey on other domestic animals. Although it has been known to catch and kill small antelopes, its diet consists mainly of birds, rodents, and tree hyraxes. The jungle cat exists on a similar diet.

DESERT SPECIALIST

The sand cat is a night hunter. Its somewhat low-set ears give it acute hearing and also help keep it more inconspicuous by rounding its outline in areas where there is little in the way of natural cover. It will crouch motionless with endless patience, waiting for small desert rodents, such as jerboas, as well as lizards and other reptiles, to draw within pouncing range. It also eats desert insects—locusts, for example. The sand cat can survive for lengthy periods without drinking, getting the bulk of the moisture it needs from the food it eats. ∎

SMALL STALKER

The tiny black-footed cat (left) uses extreme stealth when hunting rodents, lizards, and insects, catching them with a final spring.

GRASSLAND SPECIALIST

The serval (right) uses its keen hearing to tune in to the rustlings of rodents in long grass. Having pinpointed the location of the prey, it stalks and pounces.

DESERT HUNTER

There are plenty of jerboas and gerbils in the deserts of North Africa—food for the superbly camouflaged sand cat (left), which hunts them by night.

Illustration Simon Turvey/Wildlife Art Agency

TERRITORY

The African small cats occupy a basic territory in which they hunt. The size of this is variable, expanding wherever prey is scarce. African wildcats, however, can be seen in large numbers where prey is abundant—near villages, for example. Servals occupy a home range of 1–14.5 sq miles (2.7–38 sq km), although the larger home ranges may be shared with other individuals.

Most males have a larger territory than females but usually actively defend only a much smaller core area. This territory may overlap with those of several females. To avoid each other, cats scent mark trees, bushes, posts, and other landmarks around their home range.

SCENT MARKING

A cat sprays urine to warn others of its presence, rather than to defend a territory. Both sexes spray, and although males seem to do so more often, females spray more frequently when they are in estrus. One male serval was observed spraying urine up to 46 times in an hour, whereas a female did so only 15 to 20 times.

By sniffing at the scent, another cat learns about the sprayer's sex, its mating condition—if it is female—and how long ago the spot was visited. Other sources of scent are the sebaceous glands on the forehead, chin, lips, and tail. Sweat glands

DEFENSIVE CARACAL

The caracal's ears, together with facial expressions, are used to warn other caracals of its mood. They are held erect in this defensive display.

AGGRESSIVE CARACAL

With ears swept back and teeth bared, this facial expression is unmistakably aggressive.

(in)SIGHT

SCRATCH AND SPEAK

Most owners of domestic cats will be all too familiar with the way their pet rakes its claws down a suitable surface—usually the best armchair unless a scratching post is provided. Undoubtedly, this helps rid the claws of any loose or flaking pieces of nail. In the wild, however, scratching is yet another form of communication. Around their territories, cats run their claws down the bark of trees or on a fence post. The resulting scratches leave a visual sign, but there is probably also a residual smell message left by the sweat glands in the footpads.

Other cats leave scrapes and scratches in the ground. The puma, for example, often scrapes at the soil while urinating. This is presumed to serve as a signal to other pumas in the area.

SUBMISSION

Not all meetings end in a flurry of claws and fur. Most cats would rather live and let live. This jungle cat (below left) is submitting meekly to the aggressor.

In contrast to their small stature, black-footed cats have a deserved reputation for ferocity. These black-foots (right) are defending the entrance to their den.

on the soles of the feet may also be used. A cat rubs these parts of its anatomy on key bushes or even on the ground. Quite often, glandular secretions are used to anoint another cat, either a female on her kittens or a male and female on each other before they mate. During such a session, the cats will often dribble extensively, thus soaking one another in saliva as well.

CAT FIGHTS

Most confrontations between small cats involve males. A young male may challenge a senior for his territory, but fighting more usually concerns access to a mate. A male defending his property attempts to chase an intruder off, swiping out with his paws. If the intruder is determined to stand its ground, a typical fight follows. One male slowly approaches

Anthony Bannister/NHPA

the other with his fur raised and his tail twitching. The adversary rolls onto his back to use his forepaws in defense. The aggressor may well stop, withdrawing his head to avoid the strike, while at the same time lashing out with a forepaw. If a full-scale fight is to follow, the prone cat will attempt to pull the other down, and the animals are likely to roll around, each hissing and growling as they attempt to bite into the other's coat.

The serval behaves differently in confrontations. Hostile pairs have been seen racing around one another, tails arched over their backs as they leap high into the air. After this frenzy of activity, they face one another with bristling hair and arched backs, making low warning growls as they curl back their lips to bare their teeth. Eventually they lash out at one another with their forepaws. ■

B/W illustrations Ruth Grewcock

Color illustration Kim Thompson

LIFE CYCLE

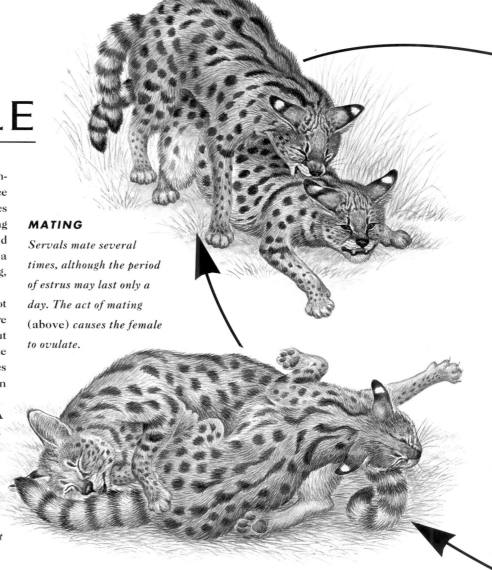

MATING

Servals mate several times, although the period of estrus may last only a day. The act of mating (above) causes the female to ovulate.

With the serval, most births occur in the summer, although females may reproduce twice in a twelve-month period. Often, the female initiates the pairing; just before she comes into breeding condition, she calls loudly to attract males and scent marks the ground copiously. Having found a suitor, she stays with him for a week or so, hunting, mating, and resting with him.

Up to four young are born in a sheltered spot after a gestation of ten to eleven weeks. They are helpless at birth, but their eyes open after about nine days, and they double their birth weight by the time they are eleven days old. The family disperses when the female breeds again, although she often drives the males away earlier than the females.

Caracals, too, usually give birth in summer. A receptive female mates over six days or so with a number of males. Having prepared a cozy nest, after a gestation of seventy to seventy-eight days, she gives birth to up to six cubs. Their eyes open between six and ten days after birth, and at just three weeks old they begin chasing prey. A week

Black-footed kittens (below) *are well developed at birth and rapidly reach independence.*

Kenneth W. Fink/Ardea

GROWING UP

The life of a young serval

LESSONS IN LIFE

As with all cats, play-fighting is more than just fun. It teaches juveniles how to defend themselves as adults (left).

BIRTH

The female gives birth (left) in dense ground cover or in the empty burrow of another animal. The kittens' soft, pale fur already shows the blurred adult markings.

abundant. Their gestation period is fifty-six to sixty days and the average litter size is four. The kittens open their eyes at about ten days old and start leaving the den when they are four weeks old. They are fully independent at five months or even earlier, for wildcats may give birth more than once a year. The young themselves are ready to breed when only a year old.

The female sand cat has a particularly loud mating call, helping her to attract a male over quite a long distance. She will give birth to a litter of two to four, after a gestation period of fifty-nine to sixty-three days. The kittens have dark tabby markings at birth, which soon fade to the sandy adult coat.

BLACK-FOOTED CATS STAY PAIRED FOR A FEW HOURS ONLY, AFTER WHICH THE FEMALE RAPIDLY SENDS THE MALE AWAY

Although the kittens are blind until two weeks old, they grow at an enormous rate. Weighing some 1.4 oz (39 g) at birth, they may gain as much as 0.4 oz (12 g) every day for the next three weeks. They do not leave the burrow until they are five weeks old. Usually the family disperses when the kittens are about four months old. Like domestic cats, sand cats can have two litters a year. ■

MILK BAR

The kittens rapidly gain weight on their mother's rich milk (above). When at last they can take solid food, she alters her routine, hunting through much of the day in order to bring them meat.

later the mother moves them each day, choosing hideaways in deep cover. They can eat meat from four to six weeks old, and they are weaned at four to six months. They leave their mother at about ten months old, in search of new territories.

For its size, the black-footed cat has a long gestation period—up to sixty-eight days—and its litter of one to three newborns are well developed compared to those of other cat species. Their eyes open within a week, and they can catch live prey four or five weeks later. At first the mother moves her kittens from the nest site every few days, but as soon as they can run well, she makes no effort to drive them into cover in the face of danger. Instead, they hide in whatever cover they can find until she gives a special "all-clear" call.

The African wildcat produces its young during the rainy period, when prey will be at its most

FROM BIRTH TO DEATH

SERVAL	CARACAL
GESTATION: 70–76 DAYS	**GESTATION:** 70–78 DAYS
LITTER SIZE: 1–4	**LITTER SIZE:** 1–6, USUALLY 2
WEIGHT AT BIRTH: 7–8.8 OZ (200–250 G)	**WEIGHT AT BIRTH:** 8.8 OZ (ABOUT 250 G)
EYES OPEN: ABOUT 9 DAYS	**EYES OPEN:** 6–9 DAYS
WEANED: 5 MONTHS	**WEANED:** 4–6 MONTHS
SEXUAL MATURITY: 1.5–2.5 YEARS	**SEXUAL MATURITY:** 1–2 YEARS
LONGEVITY: 12–17 YEARS	**LONGEVITY:** UP TO 17 YEARS

Color illustrations Robin Budden/Wildlife Art Agency

TOO SMALL TO SAVE?

THE SMALL CATS OF THE WORLD HAVE NEVER WON THE ATTENTION AFFORDED TO THE BIG CATS, EITHER IN TERMS OF PERSECUTION OR CONSERVATION. THE FUTURE OF MANY, HOWEVER, IS UNCERTAIN

Most of the big cats, particularly those with beautiful coats—the tiger, cheetah, jaguar, leopard, and snow leopard—have long been a target for hunters. Not only were they traditionally seen as prized trophies by big game hunters, but in the past there have also been fortunes to be made in the sale of their skins to the fur trade. The small cats have never shared the same limelight. Mostly very shy and secretive anyway, hunting them has never been considered sufficiently prestigious.

THE CAT COAT TRADE

In the 1960s and 1970s, realizing both the plight of the big cats and the fact that, if kept alive in reasonable numbers, they would bring in revenue in the form of tourism, those countries that were home to these animals initiated legal protection to ban hunting and trapping. Although media attention was also directed against the wearing of fur coats, there remained a demand for the skins of spotted cats by those people who valued a fur coat as the ultimate status symbol. As the supply of big cat skins dwindled, fur traders turned their attentions to the small cats. When these animals did become targets, they were killed in horrifically high numbers, for it takes many skins of the smaller cats to make a single coat.

The small cats of the New World and parts of Asia have suffered the most because of their coats. However, at one time the serval looked as if it might incur very heavy losses because of its attractive markings. For a while it became a target, particularly in East Africa, where it was widely hunted. Now, although poachers operating for the fur trade may still hunt, a strict watch is kept by customs officials for the illegal export of cats' skins from African countries. Undoubtedly, many slip through the net; policing of this nature needs

money, and many of the poorer countries become all the poorer because they believe they cannot afford to protect their natural assets.

To an extent, the serval has always been hunted by native people. Apparently it makes good eating and, at one time, natives used the skins to make fur cloaks called karosses. Today, an ambivalent attitude prevails. Some farmers and villagers see servals as pests—predators of poultry and other domestic livestock. On the other hand, these cats are supreme mousers and can do much to control rodent populations around settlements.

The plain coat of the caracal has never been thought desirable by fur traders, so this cat has not been greatly persecuted in this regard. But because

A specialist at hunting savanna rodents, the serval (right) is unfortunately also a killer of livestock.

Richard du Toit/Images of Africa

The African wildcat (above), a close cousin of the European wildcat, is faring reasonably well today.

Mike Wilkes/Aquila

THEN & NOW

This map shows the former and present distribution of the serval.

⊟ **DISTRIBUTION IN THE 19TH CENTURY**

⊟ **DISTRIBUTION 2,000–3,000 YEARS AGO**

▪ **CURRENT DISTRIBUTION**

At one time the serval occupied practically all of Africa, except for some equatorial forests and the southern tip. As the Sahara grew more arid, the species retreated in the north to occupy moister western areas, where its distribution today is fragmented. It has declined also in the extreme south. The serval is still reasonably common today in the great savanna belts of eastern and southern Africa.

it kills domestic livestock, often in high numbers, thousands of caracals have been killed in stock-farming areas. It is apparently easy to tame, and at one time it was trained and used by hunters, particularly in Iran and India, in the pursuit of other animals. Today, although it is thought to be less widespread than it once was across Africa, it is still fairly numerous. Sadly, however, this is not the case over most of its range in Asia and India, where it is extremely scarce, if not altogether absent.

THREATS TO OTHER CATS

The little sand cat has appealed to the fur trade—surprisingly, perhaps, because its markings are not as pronounced and dramatic as many of the spotted

ALONGSIDE MAN

DEITY OR DEVIL?

Mankind's fascination and association with cats goes way back into prehistory. A cat's jawbone dating from about 6,000 B.C., discovered in a human settlement in Cyprus, tells a story, for this is an island where there were no indigenous wildcats. It would appear, therefore, that cats were taken there by humans at around this time. Cats have been domesticated in Egypt for at least 4,000 years.

The relationship between humans and cats since the two came into contact has veered between one of reverence to one of intense persecution. Cats have played a key part in religion: associated with deities by some cultures, but seen in other communities as agents of the devil and favorites of witches. Above all, wherever humans have colonized, they have taken cats with them as an important part of their civilization.

cats. However, its coat is particularly thick and soft. The height of its persecution came in 1967–1972, and since this time it has become increasingly rare.

Although probably not endangered across most of its African range, the African wildcat is declining in some northern parts. Killed frequently as a raider of poultry houses, it is also subjected to "control exercises" in certain areas, because it is considered to be an important rabies vector.

Africa's Serengeti plains are home to literally millions of large mammals. Here, there is plenty of prey for large and small cats alike.

The coat of the African golden cat has not appealed widely to the fur trade, yet it was highly esteemed by native people, who considered it so valuable that they were not prepared to trade in it. Traditionally it was used to make tribal robes.

LOSING AND GAINING GROUND

Although most African small cats have escaped the attentions of the fur trade and the hunters' guns, they have lost much habitat to human settlement. In many instances, they have been driven back into small, fragmented areas, where they cannot easily find mates. This leads to inbreeding, which affects the long-term survival of any species.

Human intrusion into cat country often brings the two into conflict. Agricultural practices not only alter the land, but also attract rats and mice—and thereby also the small cats, which do not always discriminate between rodents and domestic livestock. As a result, the cats are viewed as pests.

But it is not all bad news for the small cats. Those species in Africa have benefited enormously, but probably incidentally, from the establishment of the many national parks, where visitors go on safari to see the magnificent big game animals. Because so much of Africa is home to these small, versatile cats, they have found themselves sustained and preserved within the national parks, largely protected from the gun and trap. ∎

Alan Root/Survival Anglia

INTO THE FUTURE

Because the small cats do not have the high profile of their larger relatives—the lions and cheetahs, for example—they do not have the same pulling power when it comes to attracting visitors to national parks where such animals may be seen in the wild. Consequently there have not been the same organized and influential campaigns to attempt to conserve or protect them.

In many instances the status of the small wildcats is not fully known. Their lifestyle and habits—shy, nocturnal, often living in inaccessible and inhospitable regions—makes them difficult to study. Facilities and resources are simply not available in many places to monitor even those cats that are known to be at some risk.

Studies of animals in the wild have been assisted in recent decades by the use of radiotelemetry. An animal is caught and drugged, then fitted with a

PREDICTION

THE END OF THE LINE?
The Pakistani subspecies of the African sand cat, discovered only in 1966, is close to extinction. Less than a dozen are to be found in zoos, and they have all descended from one breeding pair, so they are not good candidates for further breeding unless some outside stock can be found.

collar containing a small radio transmitter that allows its movements to be tracked. This has assisted knowledge of the habits and status of some small cats. However, most of such research has been conducted on the wildcats of the Americas rather than those of Africa or Asia.

BREEDING PROGRAMS
Obviously, zoos and captive-breeding programs, which are becoming more extensive around the world, can help with the continuation of species that are critically endangered. However, not all of the small cats breed successfully in captive conditions.

Fortunately for the servals and caracals, they are two of the African small cats that do appear to respond well to captivity and will breed relatively successfully. Servals are also said to be easy to tame and make good pets. Neither of these species, however, appear to be in any great danger in the wild. ■

SURVIVAL PLANS

Zoos around the world now cooperate extensively in captive-breeding programs, particularly since the establishment of Species Survival Plans (SSPs). Catering now to more than sixty endangered species, the idea behind this is to ensure that genetically diverse and viable populations of animals that are declining in the world survive in zoos. Small cats present a number of new challenges to zoos since many species have not been bred in captivity. SSPs help to bring practical and scientific expertise together to manage small cat species as naturally as possible. SSPs have already helped some of the world's big cats: tigers, snow leopards, and cheetahs.

THE FROZEN ZOO

At the Frozen Zoo, part of the large complex of Cincinnati Zoo in Ohio, revolutionary new experiments are taking place in the breeding of various species of wild animals. One such has involved Africa's caracal. Eggs and sperm are taken from captive female and male caracals, put together, and kept under the right conditions in a laboratory to enable them to develop into embryos. At that point, the developed embryos are surgically inserted into the uterus of a female domestic cat, with the hopes that she will give birth to a healthy caracal.

In these experiments, embryos and sperm are kept frozen until required, hence the name Frozen Zoo. Although this sort of experimentation is still in its comparative infancy, it is hoped it will increase the number of offspring that a rare animal can produce.

Illustration Sean Milne

SHREWS

RELATIONS

Shrews and solenodons belong to the order of insectivores, or Insectivora. Other members of the order include:

TENRECS

HEDGEHOGS

MOONRATS

GOLDEN MOLES

MOLES

DESMANS

OTTER SHREWS

A. & E. Bomford/Ardea

SHORT AND SHARP NOSED

SHREWS ARE SO SMALL THAT WE RARELY SEE THEM—WHICH IS IRONIC, FOR THESE TINY, POINTED BUNDLES PASS ALMOST ALL OF THEIR BRIEF EXISTENCE IN A FRENZY OF HYPERACTIVITY

A shrill squeak and a rustling in the forest's leaf litter may be the closest you will ever get to seeing a shrew in the wild. Shrews are notoriously difficult to spot, not because they are rare animals but because of their secretive and solitary nature. Even so, the tiny shrew has worked its way into popular folklore as a rather villainous, unlucky creature, capable of poisoning horses and turning cattle lame—a reputation almost wholly undeserved.

Their prey apart, shrews do very little harm to people or other animals. The shrews' reputation, sadly, is based on the mystery surrounding their habits.

· Shrews are small and mouselike, with pointed snouts and short, thick fur. They range in size from the tiny Etruscan pygmy shrew, which weighs in at 0.07 oz (2 g) and is the smallest terrestrial mammal in the world, to the much larger water shrews, which are about the size of rats. They and their cousins, the solenodons, are insectivores—mammals whose

CLASSIFICATION

Shrews and solenodons are insect-eating mammals, belonging to the order of insectivores. This order is split into six families. Shrews belong to the Soricidae family and Solenodons to the Solenodontidae family.

ORDER

Insectivora
(insectivores)

FAMILY

Soricidae
(shrews)
266 species in 20 genera

LARGEST GENERA

Crocidura
117 species
Sorex
52 species

FAMILY

Solenodontidae
(solenodons)
2 species in 1 genus

SPECIES

Solenodon paradoxus
(Hispaniola solenodon)
Solenodon cubanus
(Cuban solenodon

diet is based mainly on insects and other small invertebrates. Of the 345 species of insectivores, some two-thirds are shrews, with new species being discovered on a regular basis. Solenodons are the size of large shrews, with very long, flexible snouts, which they use for probing into nooks and crannies for food. They are some of the largest insectivores, weighing up to 2.2 lb (1 kg).

An ancient lineage

Shrews are among the most ancient of mammals, although the tiny size of their bones and teeth make it difficult for zoologists to unravel their evolutionary history. They originated in Europe early in the Eocene epoch, about fifty-four million years ago. They have lived in America for thirty-eight million years and in Asia for seven million years. Early shrews were very similar to their modern-day descendants, except for a small difference in size. For example, about two million years ago, the European common shrew and the pygmy shrew, both of which are known from fossils, were slightly larger than they are today. Solenodons evolved about thirty million years ago; fossils of their ancestors have been found in North America.

Today, shrews are extremely abundant. They are among the most adaptable of all mammals, able

TREE SHREWS

Tree shrews are a family of insectivores of Southeast Asia. They are not strictly related to shrews and are only superficially similar in appearance and diet. There are five genera containing eighteen species, most of which live on the island of Borneo. Many are squirrel-like in form, with a bushy, tufted tail and prominent eyes. Indeed, their Malaysian name *tupai* means "squirrel."

Tree shrews inhabit tropical deciduous forests, where they nest at night in the branches or roots of trees, in hollow logs, or in ground burrows. Five long, curved claws on each foot help them to scamper about the branches with ease. They eat more or less whatever they can find—plant or animal—but above all favor insects and other invertebrates.

Unlike true shrews, some tree shrews are social, forming pair bonds or even groups. Like many mammals that live in the tropics, they may breed all year round, but they tend to produce small litters.

Joe Blossom/NHPA

Barrie E. Watts/Oxford Scientific Films

The African musk shrews (left) *include the world's largest shrews.*

The common European shrew (above) *is abundant in Great Britain's hedgerows and grasslands.*

to thrive in almost any climate and terrain. Most shrews are terrestrial, but some have adapted to life in the water, having developed webbed or fringed feet to help them swim and dive. They live a solitary life, vigorously defending their feeding territories and seeking company only when breeding.

Shrews are voracious feeders on both plant and animal matter. Several species have a poisonous bite, enabling them to kill prey larger than themselves. With tiny, ineffective eyes, they rely heavily on their senses of smell and hearing to track their

in SIGHT

SMALLEST OF ALL

The world's smallest terrestrial mammal is Savi's pygmy shrew, *Suncus etruscus*, also known as the Etruscan shrew. Adults weigh just 0.07 oz (2 g) and measure 1.4–2 in (36–51 mm) along the head and body, with a further 1 in (25 mm) of tail. This diminutive creature is so small it can squeeze down tunnels made by earthworms or beetles. It is found in grasslands and forests around the Mediterranean, in Africa as far south as South Africa, and in Asia as far east as Malaysia. Another shrew holds the record for being the smallest freshwater mammal. The southern water shrew, *Neomys anomalus*, weighs 0.3–0.6 oz (8.5–17 g) and is 4–6 in (102–152 mm) long.

prey. They use a wide range of squeaks, clicks, and screams, mainly for communication and, possibly, as a crude form of echolocation.

For their size, shrews have gargantuan appetites. They consume roughly their body weight in food in each twenty-four-hour period, and must eat regularly every two to three hours, simply to stay alive. This is because they have a phenomenally high metabolic rate—their tiny hearts pump at around twenty beats per second—they have an extremely high volume-to-surface area ratio, and they lose relatively more heat than larger animals. This heat must be constantly regenerated through feeding.

ISLAND SOIL SEARCHERS

Solenodons are limited to two islands in the Caribbean: Cuba and Hispaniola (the island that comprises Haiti and the Dominican Republic). Very little is known about their lifestyle, and they are now extremly rare (see Solenodons, page 2052).

Both species live in remote forest regions and are nocturnal. They mainly eat invertebrates, which they find in the soil or among the leaf litter. They rummage with their long, flexible snouts, grubbing up and catching prey with their huge, strong claws. Like shrews, solenodons rely on their senses of smell, hearing, and touch to find their prey and use a venomous bite to kill it. They are equipped with scent glands, which give off a goaty odor. Unlike shrews, which usually live for little over a year in the wild, solenodons can reach the ripe old age of six. However, they have a low reproductive rate and give birth to small litters, two factors that contribute to their increasing rarity. ∎

TRUE SHREWS?

The order Insectivora was first introduced in 1816 to classify and group together shrews, moles, and hedgehogs. A year later, the order was extended to include tenrecs, golden moles, and desmans. Later still, with the addition of tree shrews, elephant shrews, and animals that did not seem to fit anywhere else, the insectivore order became a mixed bag of somewhat disparate species.

Today, the order is more focused: Elephant shrews and colugos now have their own separate orders—Macroscelididae and Dermoptera respectively. Tree shrews, too, first classed as insectivores, then as primates, now form their own order, *Scandentia* (see Tree Shrews, page 2032).

Color illustrations Steve Kingston

B/W illustrations Ruth Grewcock

THE SOLENODON'S AND SHREW'S FAMILY TREE

There are more than 370 species in the order Insectivora. These can be divided into three suborders: Erinacoemorpha (hedgehog-type insectivores), Tenrecomorpha (tenrec-type insectivores), and Soricomorpha (shrewlike insectivores). Shrews and solenodons, together with moles and desmans, belong to the suborder Soricomorpha; they represent the largest and smallest families of insectivores.

HISPANIOLAN SOLENODON

Solenodon paradoxus
(*so-LEEN-o-don pah-rah-DOCK-suss*)

Two species of solenodons, live on the islands of Hispaniola and Cuba in the Caribbean. They are about the size of a rat, with a long snout and large, fully clawed feet. They are now both endangered as a result of predation by introduced species.

MOLES

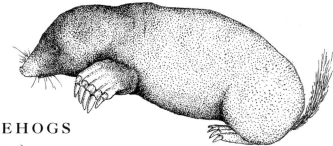

HEDGEHOGS

SUBORDER
ERINACEOMORPHA

MOON-RATS

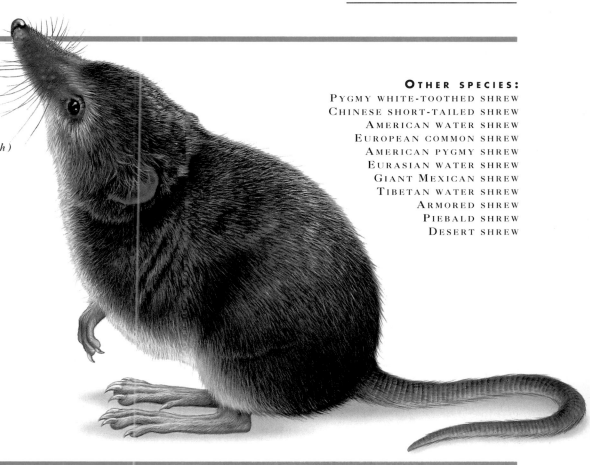

PYGMY SHREW

Sorex minuta
(soh-rex mih-NEWT-uh)

There are tinier shrews in the world, but the minuscule European pygmy shrew, found in Great Britain, is one of the tinier shrews in the world. It reaches a total of 4.3 in (11 cm), including the tail, and weighs up to about 0.2 oz (6 g). It is, however, an adaptable and resilient creature, recorded as living even on Ben Nevis, Scotland's highest mountain.

OTHER SPECIES:
PYGMY WHITE-TOOTHED SHREW
CHINESE SHORT-TAILED SHREW
AMERICAN WATER SHREW
EUROPEAN COMMON SHREW
AMERICAN PYGMY SHREW
EURASIAN WATER SHREW
GIANT MEXICAN SHREW
TIBETAN WATER SHREW
ARMORED SHREW
PIEBALD SHREW
DESERT SHREW

TENRECS

SUBORDER
SORICOMORPHA

GOLDEN MOLE

SUBORDER
TENRECOMORPHA

INSECTIVORES

ⒶNCESTORS

MEGAZOSTRODON

The first true mammals appeared on Earth about 200 million years ago. They were tiny creatures, similar in appearance to large shrews, and, like shrews, they fed mainly on insects. They probably hunted at night to avoid being preyed on by the day-hunting dinosaurs. One of the best-known prehistoric mammals, the ancestors of today's shrews, was *Megazostrodon*, known to have lived in South Africa. These first mammals evolved from reptiles and may have laid eggs, like reptiles, rather than giving birth to live young.

ANATOMY: THE SHREW

The smallest shrew, Savi's pymgy shrew (above left), has a head-and-body length of 1.4–2 in (36–51 mm), with a tail 1–1.2 in (25–30 mm) long. The largest shrew, the African forest shrew (above center), has a head-and-body length of 6 in (152 mm). The Hispaniolan solenodon (above right) is 11–13 in (280–330 mm) long from snout to rump, with a tail length of 8.5–10 in (216–254 mm).

THE COAT

is short and thick. In most shrews, the fur is brown or gray. Shrews that live in colder climates have longer, thicker fur than those found in warmer regions.

THE EYES

are small, largely hidden by fur, and provide poor eyesight. Shrews also have small ears, although their hearing is excellent.

WHISKERS

on the head and snout help the animal navigate and find its prey. They are also used in confrontations between strangers.

GROUND-DWELLING SHREW

CLIMBING SHREW

SEMIAQUATIC SHREW

FEET

Insectivores have five toes and claws on each foot. Solenodons use their huge claws to dig and tear open rotten branches for food. Climbing shrews have dexterous toes for gripping branches. Water shrews have larger, broader feet than land-based shrews, with toes fringed with hairs to give their feet a greater surface area for paddling and pushing through the water. The feet of the Tibetan water shrew have evolved even further: This is the only species of shrew with truly webbed feet.

TEETH

The Soricidae family of shrews is divided into two groups based on their teeth. Red-toothed shrews, such as the European common shrew, have red tips to their teeth. White-toothed shrews have pure white teeth. Solenodons have grooves in their lower incisor teeth, down which their venom flows as they bite into prey.

incisor   molars and premolars

COMMON SHREW SKULL

pincer-action incisors

The primitive skull shape is typical of insectivores, with a small braincase and long jaws. The incisors are prominent: In the shrew they project to

SOLENODON SKULL

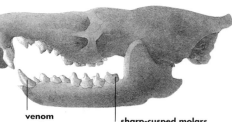

venom teeth   sharp-cusped molars

form a beak, while in the solenodon the massive upper incisor is angled backward. The crowns of the molars have sharp cusps for crunching insects.

X-ray illustrations Elisabeth Smith

WATER SHREW

COMMON SHREW

WHITE-TOOTHED SHREW

TAIL SHAPES

The shrew's tail is covered with short bristles. Shrews' tails lose their hair with age. Some species have naked tails; others store fat in their tails for times when food is scarce.

THE BODY

is typically cylindrical. The shrew's compact, tubular form enables it to push efficiently through undergrowth and to squeeze into narrow tunnels to escape predators.

THE FEET

have long bones. Shrews walk wholly or partially on their soles; solenodons, however, use only their toes when in motion.

Main illustration Barry Croucher/Wildlife Art Agency

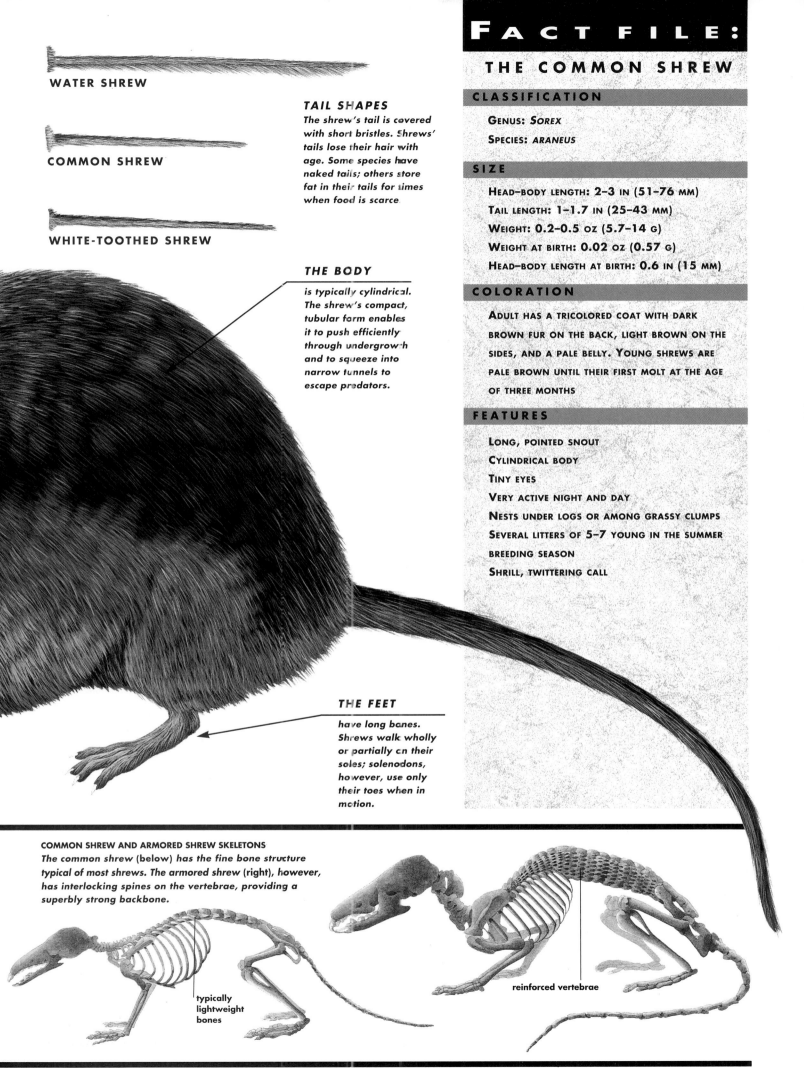

FACT FILE:

THE COMMON SHREW

CLASSIFICATION

GENUS: *SOREX*

SPECIES: *ARANEUS*

SIZE

HEAD–BODY LENGTH: 2–3 IN (51–76 MM)
TAIL LENGTH: 1–1.7 IN (25–43 MM)
WEIGHT: 0.2–0.5 OZ (5.7–14 G)
WEIGHT AT BIRTH: 0.02 OZ (0.57 G)
HEAD–BODY LENGTH AT BIRTH: 0.6 IN (15 MM)

COLORATION

ADULT HAS A TRICOLORED COAT WITH DARK BROWN FUR ON THE BACK, LIGHT BROWN ON THE SIDES, AND A PALE BELLY. YOUNG SHREWS ARE PALE BROWN UNTIL THEIR FIRST MOLT AT THE AGE OF THREE MONTHS

FEATURES

LONG, POINTED SNOUT
CYLINDRICAL BODY
TINY EYES
VERY ACTIVE NIGHT AND DAY
NESTS UNDER LOGS OR AMONG GRASSY CLUMPS
SEVERAL LITTERS OF 5–7 YOUNG IN THE SUMMER BREEDING SEASON
SHRILL, TWITTERING CALL

COMMON SHREW AND ARMORED SHREW SKELETONS
The common shrew (below) has the fine bone structure typical of most shrews. The armored shrew (right), however, has interlocking spines on the vertebrae, providing a superbly strong backbone.

typically lightweight bones

reinforced vertebrae

LIFE IN THE FAST LANE

SHREWS ARE BASICALLY SOLITARY; WITH A LIFESTYLE CENTERED AROUND THE LIFE-OR-DEATH BUSINESS OF FEEDING, THEY HAVE PRECIOUS LITTLE TIME FOR SOCIAL ACTIVITY—OR, INDEED, FOR ANYTHING ELSE

Active day and night, a shrew's life is a constant round of hunting for food, resting, and hunting for food again. In its pursuit of prey, the shrew forages ceaselessly through the undergrowth, snout quivering and ears pricked, alert to the sound of stoats, weasels, polecats, and other predators.

The shrew fiercely defends a patch of forest or grassland from intruders, to ensure that its territory and its food supply remains its own. So precious is the food supply that fights are commonplace, rapidly turning into noisy wrestling matches if the trespasser does not retreat. Otherwise a shrew is normally a solitary creature—except for a short spell during the breeding season—living and hunting alone, preserving its energy for the task at hand.

TOUR OF DUTY

Some shrews hunt along established pathways created by other small mammals, such as voles. Others seem to have no set route. They scurry hither and thither through the leaf litter and undergrowth, on the lookout for anything that might be edible.

A shrew's daily life follows a fairly set pattern. Common and pygmy shrews have a three-hourly rhythm of feeding and resting. They rest in grass and leaf nests hidden under logs or among clumps of grass, sleeping on their bellies with their feet and tails tucked underneath. They only sleep deeply for very short periods; the rest of the time is spent grooming and cleaning their fur and tidying or repairing the nest. These sleeping nests are smaller than the nests used by mother shrews caring for their young. Although active both day and night, shrews seem to have peaks of activity between dusk and dawn and in the early morning. Shrews do not hibernate, but are active summer and winter alike, searching for food.

Water shrews are no less busy than their ground-living relatives. Most can swim and dive well, equipped with water-repellent fur and ears that can be battened down with a tiny flap of skin. They, too, take regular rests between feeding forays, retiring every few hours to their riverbank burrows.

SECRETIVE SOLENODONS

Very little is known about the behavior or lifestyle of solenodons. Unlike shrews, these creatures are strictly nocturnal, using their keen senses of touch, smell, and hearing to guide them in the darkness. They forage through the vegetation on the forest floor, chirping and squeaking as they go.

During the day, solenodons rest and sleep inside hollow tree trunks, under logs, in caves, or in holes in the ground. They do not build a sleeping nest from vegetation, but sometimes dig burrow systems in the soil, seeking both shelter and prey in these

Barrie E. Watts/Oxford Scientific Films

A pygmy shrew licks its anus (above)—*an activity that probably provides it with extra nutrients.*

When diving for prey, the water shrew (left) *propels itself mainly with its fringed hind feet.*

Daniel Heuclin/NHPA

The greater white-toothed shrew (above) *sinks its teeth into a meal.*

hidden networks. They only emerge from their lairs at night, waddling jerkily through the forest in a zigzag manner, rarely in a straight line. They are clumsy movers and are apparently prone to tripping over their own feet—particularly when scurrying away from an enemy. Solenodons seem to enjoy bathing, and, when taking a dip in a forest stream, will use the occasion to drink. It may be that, with such a long snout, quenching a thirst is otherwise difficult to accomplish.

Once, the solenodons were predators with little to fear on their Caribbean island homes. Today, however, their peace is regularly disturbed. Over the last few centuries, with the successive arrivals of European settlers, introduced species such as rats, cats, and mongooses have jumped ship and settled on Cuba and Hispaniola. Worse still, solenodons seem to be vulnerable even to their own venom. Studies in captivity show that these insectivores attack their own kind with little hesitation, and fatalities can result from even the slightest flesh wound.

Consequently, a solenodon's daily routine is fraught with danger. Frequently aggressive to other individuals of its species, and savage in its attacks upon prey, it nevertheless falls prey to many opportunistic killers that were absent from its habitat during its evolutionary history. Cats and other enemies rarely eat solenodons, owing to the rank odor exuded from the scent glands in their armpits and groin, but they will kill it nonetheless. ■

Stephen Dalton/NHPA

HABITATS

Shrews are highly successful mammals, widely distributed throughout the world. They are found in Europe, Asia, Africa, North America, and Central America. Several species are also found in the far northwest of South America. There are no shrews in Australia, New Zealand, the Arctic, and Antarctic, nor in the West Indies.

Although some shrews are good climbers or burrowers, most are terrestrial, occupying habitats such as woods, grasslands, and forests. But shrews have proved extremely hardy and adaptable. They are found in a wide range of environments, both tropical and temperate, and even on windy mountain slopes, the icy nothern tundra, and in hot deserts.

Some shrews—for example, the so-called house shrew of southern Europe—seem quite at home in people's yards, sheds, and compost heaps. Similar species live around landfills in parts of Asia and Africa, where they provide a useful service by feeding on the cockroaches that amass around the garbage.

THE SCILLY SHREW

One species with very limited distribution is the Scilly shrew, or lesser white-toothed shrew. Within the British Isles, it occurs only on the Scilly and Channel islands. It prefers the seaside, where it preys on sand fleas, beetles, and flies, and can be

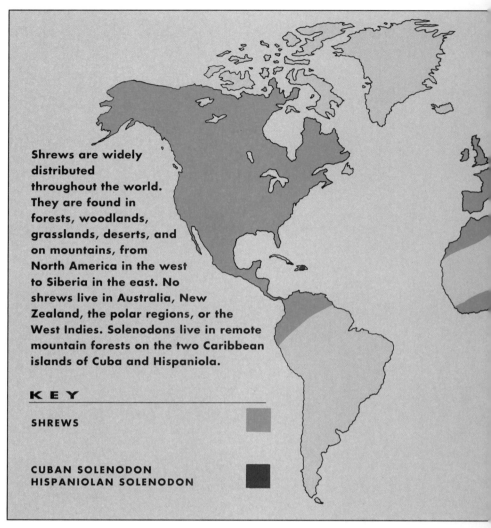

Shrews are widely distributed throughout the world. They are found in forests, woodlands, grasslands, deserts, and on mountains, from North America in the west to Siberia in the east. No shrews live in Australia, New Zealand, the polar regions, or the West Indies. Solenodons live in remote mountain forests on the two Caribbean islands of Cuba and Hispaniola.

KEY

SHREWS

CUBAN SOLENODON
HISPANIOLAN SOLENODON

C. & T. Stuart/Natural Science Photos

DISTRIBUTION

Barrie E. Watts/Oxford Scientific Films

in SIGHT

HOT AND COLD SHREWS

Being tiny, shrews are able to adapt to microclimates, limited habitats with their own unique environmental conditions. Some species, such as desert shrews, can survive in the desert, where both food and water are scarce, by lowering their metabolic rates. These are called cold shrews. Other shrews, which live in colder climates, are able to raise their body temperatures to survive. They are called hot shrews.

found among the clumps of seaweed on the shore or up on the sand dunes. No one is quite sure how the Scilly shrew reached the islands; one theory suggests that it was introduced in the Iron Age by tin traders from continental Europe.

SPECIALIZED SHREWS

Shrews share the same basic body plan and physical characteristics, but some have become specialized to suit particular habitats. Water shrews, as we have seen, have broad feet with fringed toes to help them swim; they are equally at home in the water and on land. The European water shrew also has extra hairs on the underside of its tail. This species inhabits unpolluted, fast-flowing streams and rivers, particularly beside watercress

A musk shrew devours a beetle (left). *There are some fifteen species of musk shrews in the forests, scrubland, and savanna of Africa.*

The tiny pygmy shrew (right) *is distributed over a massive range, from all of Europe eastward to Siberia and China.*

beds, although it also occurs in ponds and ditches. Fringed toes are also a specialty of the Turkestan desert shrew. Its feet are edged with long, stiff hairs that help it keep a firm grip on the shifting sand and dig into it if it needs to make a quick getaway. Escape routes are important to all shrews, to help them flee from owls and other birds of prey. Accordingly, some ground cover, such as low vegetation, is essential in a habitat. This also offers shrews a variety of secure sites for their sleeping and breeding nests. Some shrews rest and shelter in burrows already excavated by other small mammals, while others dig their own underground tunnel systems. And of course, because shrews need to eat so much and so regularly, their chosen habitat must contain a plentiful supply of food.

Several different species of shrews may be found in any one habitat. In a European forest, for example, one might expect to find European common shrews, pygmy shrews, and European water shrews all living together. Numbers increase in places such as African swamps, where up to twenty-five species might be found in one location.

DEMISE IN PUERTO RICO

In contrast to the abundance of the shrews, the solenodons are limited to remote mountain forests

FOCUS ON

THE WELSH STREAM

From the Brecon Beacons north to Snowdonia, the Welsh heartland is characterized by rolling green countryside flanked by dramatic mountain ranges, relics of both volcanic and glacial activity. Much of Wales's high rainfall drains to the coast by highly fragmented routes, so the area is rich in rivers and streams flowing through green valleys. The European water shrew lives along the banks of the rivers, streams, and lakes, where it swims and dives for insect larvae, fish, and frogs.

This shrew's toes, fingers, and tail are fringed with stiff hairs, increasing their surface area and making them more effective paddles in the water. It also has thick, water-repellant fur to prevent its coat becoming waterlogged and an extra layer of fat to insulate it and keep it warm in the chilly stream water. This waterproof fur traps bubbles of air, which appear underwater as a silvery "jacket" on the shrew. The trapped air gives the shrew extra buoyancy.

The water shrew dives for up to twenty seconds at a time; it carries prey back to land before eating it. It is one of several species of shrews with a poisonous bite, injecting its venom into its victim's neck; the poison acts on the nervous system, causing paralysis.

TEMPERATURE AND RAINFALL

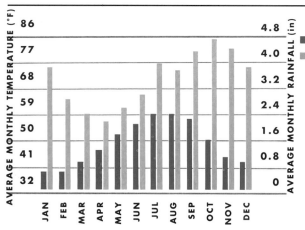

Affected chiefly by Atlantic air masses, the Welsh climate is varied. The average annual rainfall is 55 in (1,400 mm). The annual mean temperature is 50°F (10°C).

on Cuba and Hispaniola. They spend their time on the forest floor, where there is plenty of food to be found, and they can also climb trees. Solenodons were once also found on the island of Puerto Rico. As on the other Caribbean islands, however, introduced species such as dogs, rats, and mongooses preyed on the solenodons and competed with them for food supplies. This, combined with rapid forest clearance to provide space for human settlements, has meant that the solenodons of Puerto Rico are now almost extinct. ∎

NEIGHBORS

Rivers, streams, and lakes are sources of food and shelter for a wide variety of animals—fish, birds, reptiles, crustaceans, mammals, amphibians, and many microscopic creatures.

RED KITE

This rare bird of prey, with its deeply forked tail, lives in Welsh oak woods, where it preys on small mammals.

TROUT

Trout can be found in rivers, lakes, and oceans. They lay their eggs in winter on gravel riverbeds.

Illustrations Dan Wright

WALES

Much of the Welsh terrain is dominated by the broad spine of the Cambrian mountain range, which links Snowdonia National Park with the southern counties of Glamorgan and Dyfed. The mountain peaks and slopes are rugged and bleak, but the lowland valleys are lush, forested refuges for wildlife.

SNOWDONIA

CAMBRIANS

Stephen Dalton/NHPA

HEDGEHOG	**VOLE**	**FROG**	**RED FOX**	**OTTER**

Insectivores like shrews, hedgehogs come out at night to feed on slugs and earthworms.	Water voles burrow in river-banks. Expert swimmers, they escape enemies by diving into the water.	The frog's skin needs to be kept damp, so it stays close to water, hiding in marginal vegetation.	Red foxes are opportunists: They prey on shrews and other small mammals, and almost everything else.	The sleek otter hunts for fish, detecting them with its whiskers and keen eyesight. It eats its catch in the water.

FOOD AND FEEDING

Shrews and solenodons feed mainly on insects, although they do eat other invertebrates such as earthworms, slugs, and snails. Indeed, shrews will eat almost anything they can find or catch, adapting to whatever prey is locally available. For example, water shrews catch and kill frogs, small fish, and aquatic invertebrates; desert shrews hunt for lizards in the sand. A little plant matter, such as seeds and nuts, is an essential addition to a shrew's diet.

As a result of their high metabolism, shrews need to eat as soon as they have digested their last meal, and they may feed up to ten times within twenty-four hours. Their diet is, weight for weight, less nutritious than that eaten by rodents of the same size; as a result, shrews need to make up in

> EUROPEAN COMMON AND PYGMY SHREWS HAVE A PREFERENCE FOR WOOD LICE IN THEIR DIET BUT REJECT MILLIPEDES

bulk what is lacking in nutritional quality. They fiercely defend their food sources from intruders. If they do not, they may quickly starve to death.

Scarcity of food is not the only cause of starvation. A shrew has two sets of teeth throughout its lifetime, but, since the first set is reabsorbed while it is still in the womb, it is born with the second set already in place. If these teeth wear excessively, the shrew cannot feed and consquently faces the danger of starvation. The extent of the wear on a shrew's teeth is an effective indicator of its age.

A CONSTANT QUEST

The majority of a shrew's short life is spent foraging for food under and on the surface of the carpet of leaf litter on the forest floor. Shrews rely heavily on their senses of smell, hearing, and touch to locate their prey. They may also use a basic form of echolocation, similar to that used by bats, by emitting a series of high-pitched squeaks and listening for the echoes to inform them about the whereabouts of prey or of obstacles in their paths. Solenodons, too, are likely to use echolocation.

Some shrews dig insects and insect larvae out of the ground, using their snouts and forefeet as spades. The European common shrew stores food while it is plentiful; it caches it in tunnels in the soil, ready for a time when food is more scarce or competition for food is fiercer than usual. White-toothed shrews are particularly voracious. Studies in captivity reveal that, in addition to invertebrates and

Illustration John Morris/Wildlife Art Agency

EARTHMOVER

A solenodon uses its long, mobile snout to excavate the soil and leaf litter in its search for prey (above).

DIET OF WORMS

Among insects and other invertebrates, earthworms (right) are a favorite for the common shrew. This hunter can sniff out prey buried up to 4.7 in (12 cm) in the soil.

Joe McDonald/Oxford Scientific Films

(in)SIGHT

A DEADLY DELIVERY

Solenodons and several species of shrews are the only mammals with venomous bites. They inject the venom usually through grooved teeth as they bite into the victim's neck. The venom, produced by the salivary glands, acts on the victim's respiratory, nervous, and circulatory systems. The American short-tailed shrew and the European water shrew both produce venom; that of the short-tailed shrew is potent enough to kill 200 mice and causes pain even in humans.

The production of venom enables shrews and solenodons to catch and kill prey larger than themselves, which would otherwise be beyond their reach.

PREY

Once a shrew has tracked down its prey, it pounces and pins it to the ground with its forefeet. It kills it with a well-aimed bite, then rapidly eats it.

GRASSHOPPER

BEETLES AND LARVAE

WOOD LICE

amphibians, they will also eat small mammals. When eating a mouse, for example, the white-toothed shrew always starts with the brain, then moves on to devour all of its victim except for the tail, pelt, and parts of the limbs.

SHREWS CONTRIBUTE GREATLY TO ECOSYSTEMS BY BREAKING DOWN ANIMAL TISSUE AND RETURNING IT TO THE SOIL

One curious shrew practice is that of refection, which literally means "eating again." Shrews have been observed reaching back with the head to lick the anus, which causes the rectum to project and exude a milky fluid. This behavior is thought to provide shrews with useful nutrients, and possibly also vitamins B and K, which might otherwise be difficult to obtain.

CARIBBEAN HUNTERS

The solenodons' diet includes insects such as crickets and beetles, insect larvae, earthworms, termites, millipedes, and the occasional small bird or reptile. They will even attack and devour poultry.

Solenodons hunt at night in the forest. Like shrews, they use their keen senses of touch, smell, and hearing to locate their prey. A solenodon uses its long, flexible snout to root among the leaf litter for food and to probe for prey in cracks and crevices under rocks or inside rotting logs. It catches small prey by lunging at it and pinning it down with its snout and sharp foreclaws. Scooping it up in its mouth, the solenodon then paralyzes its victim with a venomous bite. ∎

SOCIAL STRUCTURE

Except for a short period during the mating season, and for the initial period of care that a mother shrew or solenodon shows toward her young, these secretive creatures prefer to live alone. Perhaps the constant quest for food leaves them little time for anything else. There are, however, exceptions to every rule. European common shrews sometimes form small family groups, and there is even a report of a mass migration involving hundreds of water shrews. There is also evidence of social behavior among American least shrews: Several adults may share a nest and help each other dig underground tunnels. One shrew digs while another pushes the soil to the side.

TINY BUT TERRITORIAL

Many species of shrews forage within a set territory, which they defend against intruders. The sizes of territories vary among the different species—the European common shrew, for example, defends a patch of forest of about 5,380 square feet (500 square meters). Territories also vary in size according to the seasons and the location. They are larger in winter than in summer, and larger in more open, grassy areas than in more secluded, wooded areas.

Home ranges are established while the shrews are still very young. The young are encouraged to leave the nest early, to leave room for the mother's next litter. They have to find and establish their own territory and learn all they can about the best

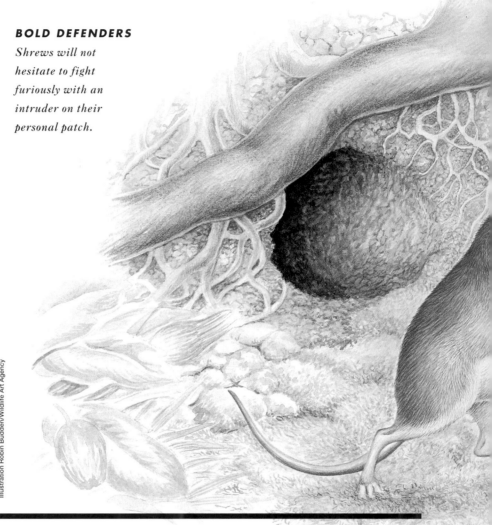

BOLD DEFENDERS

Shrews will not hesitate to fight furiously with an intruder on their personal patch.

Illustration Robin Budden/Wildlife Art Agency

NESTS AND TUNNELS

Philip Sharpe/Oxford Scientific Films

Some shrews dig underground tunnel systems, which form the foundations of their home ranges and territories. Tunnels are used for nesting, caching food, and probably avoiding predators. The European water shrew also uses its riverbank tunnels for squeezing water from its fur after a swim or dive. This helps to keep its fur in good condition.

Tunneling shrews build their grass, leaf, and moss nests in chambers off the main tunnels, here they rest between feeding bouts. Other shrews build their sleeping nests above ground, under logs, or among vegetation. The European common shrew will even climb into a bush to take over the abandoned nest of a harvest mouse.

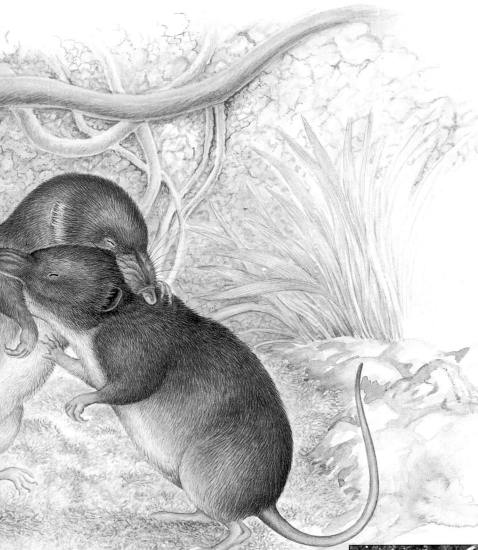

heads, bellies, or tails. Eventually, the resident drives away its adversary, chasing it off with a few well-placed bites. Many fights result in serious injuries, some even in death.

SCENT AND SOUND

Within the fixed limits of its territory, a shrew wanders widely on its daily search for food. As it roams, it marks the boundaries of its domain with droppings, urine, and secretions from its many scent glands. The scent marks pass on information about the owner to any would-be intruders, encouraging them to stay away. But scent is also used to advertise a shrew's breeding condition to a potential mate. Different species of shrews produce different scents so that they can recognize each other.

Shrews communicate more directly with sound, adapting a wide range of squeaks, clicks, twitters, and screams to suit each occasion. The European common shrew, for example, twitters softly when foraging or calling to its young and utters a repeated, peeping tone when alarmed. There is some evidence that the high-pitched screams made by two battling shrews convey information about each other's fitness and fighting abilities, thereby helping to restore the peace before blood is shed.

Solenodons also use sound, grunting, chirping, and squeaking when angry or startled. Two individuals often fight if they meet by chance, but in some cases one will establish dominance over the other, leading to an uneasy truce. ■

Graphic evidence (below) *that a shrew's pugnacity toward others is out of all proportion to its size.*

places within the territory to forage and nest. The firstborn shrews establish territories close to the nest where they were born. Members of later litters have to disperse more widely to find space. The farther afield they go, the more vulnerable they are to attack from predators. Some young shrews take over already established ranges, vacated when their older owners died. Water shrews establish their territories along riverbanks, usually along a stretch 65–300 ft (20–90 m) long. A territory also includes the zone of water just off the riverbank. Young water shrews are quite adventurous in setting up their territories, often ranging several miles from their birthplaces.

Shrews are pugnaciously territorial. If a shrew meets an intruder on its patch, both animals freeze motionless. Then the resident shrew rears up on its hind legs and screams, before chasing and attacking the intruder. The two lock together in combat, rolling around and snatching bites at each other's

Strutter Enterprises Inc./Oxford Scientific Films

LIFE CYCLE

In temperate climates, shrews breed from March to November. In the Tropics, the breeding season extends throughout the year. This is the only occasion in which shrews deliberately seek out each other's company. In the buildup to mating, shrews find suitable mates largely by scent. Then the male follows the female, chasing her and sniffing her until they finally mate. If the female is not ready to mate, she squeaks loudly and bites the male until he is driven away.

In most shrew species, the male plays no further part in the birth or care of the young after mating. He simply wanders off to find other mates. In a few species, however, the male not only helps the female to build a nest, but guards the litter while she is out on hunting trips. The breeding nest is larger and more elaborate than resting and sleeping nests. It is made from grass, leaves, and moss and may be situated in an underground chamber, in a clump of grass, or under a log.

A PRECARIOUS START

Gestation in the European common shrew lasts for about twenty-four days. Usually five to seven young are born, and a female may have two or even three litters in a season. There may be as many as fifteen young in the litters of water shrews. The newborn are naked, blind, and helpless. Some of the litter inevitably perish, often because the mother simply has too few teats to cater to all. Depending on the species, female shrews have between six and ten teats.

THE ADULT *female is receptive only for a few hours in each estrous cycle, and the brief act of mating induces her to ovulate.*

UPON REACHING *independence (twenty-five days), the young are driven away aggressively by the female, who will soon be preparing for her next litter.*

A CARAVAN OF SHREWS

Young shrews use a most effective method of staying in touch with their mothers on foraging trips, or if they are forced to abandon their nest. The first youngster grips the fur on its mother's rump in its teeth. The next baby grabs hold of the first, and before long there is a wriggling line of shrews. However fast the mother runs, the young keep up and keep in step. If the coast is clear, the shrews soon scatter to forage. But if danger appears, they form a line again and dash for safety.

YOUNG SHREWS *on the move grip on tight; if the mother is picked up, they come, too, still hanging on to her rump.*

Illustrations Simon Turvey/Wildlife Art Agency

GROWING UP

The life of a young shrew

GESTATION

lasts about three weeks, and the young remain in their burrow nest for five to eight weeks. If they stray, the mother picks them up with her mouth and carefully returns them.

AT THREE WEEKS

of age, the young are encouraged to leave the burrow on short foraging trips.

The youngsters develop very quickly. For the first week of their lives, they suckle their mother's milk. After about ten days, their fur has started to grow, and from two weeks old their eyes open. They remain in the nest, crying out to the female when hungry. She guards them closely, fending off intruders or moving to a new location if danger threatens. At the age of about eighteen days, the young shrews leave the nest for the first time. A week later, they are fully weaned and completely independent. They must then establish their own territories and forage for food by themselves. Their

FROM BIRTH TO DEATH

EUROPEAN COMMON SHREW
BREEDING SEASON: MARCH–AUGUST
GESTATION: 24–25 DAYS
LITTER SIZE: USUALLY 5–7
NUMBER OF LITTERS PER YEAR: 1–2
BODY LENGTH AT BIRTH: 0.6 IN (15 MM)
WEIGHT AT BIRTH: 0.018 OZ (0.5 G)
EYES FULLY OPEN: 16 DAYS
WEANING: 25 DAYS
SEXUAL MATURITY: 4–6 MONTHS
LONGEVITY: 12–13 MONTHS IN WILD;
UP TO 18 MONTHS IN CAPTIVITY

mother drives them out if they are unwilling to go, since she needs the nest for her next litter.

Most shrews are born in June, July, and August. They start looking for a mate the following spring, but by autumn they will die. One of the shortest lived of all mammals, most shrews live for only a year or so in the wild, although some species can live for up to four years in captivity. Some fall prey to predators, such as foxes, or owls and other birds of prey. Others starve as their teeth wear down, and a few are killed in the violent fights over territories. But a few simply die of old age and the chill of autumn.

Solenodons have a low rate of reproduction, producing perhaps two litters in a season with one or two young in each. The female gives birth in a nest burrow, where she suckles and keeps guard over her offspring. The young remain with their mother for several months; among insectivores, this represents a remarkably long period of parental care. ■

(in)SIGHT

TEAT TRANSPORTATION

Until they are about two months old, young solenodons accompany their mother on her evening hunting trips. They travel by an unusual manner, hanging on to her teats with their mouths. The female's teats are situated on her rump, and, to begin with, she simply drags her charges along with her. Later, they walk by her side, learning to recognize good foraging routes and to find food for themselves. The female will also use teat transportation if her nesting burrow is disturbed and she needs to move the vulnerable young to a safer site.

FIGHTING FOR SURVIVAL

IN THE HEART OF THE CARIBBEAN, FERAL CATS AND DOGS ARE PREYING ON THE REMAINING SOLENODONS, IN THE FINAL CHAPTER OF A HISTORY OF RUTHLESS PERSECUTION THAT BEGAN HUNDREDS OF YEARS AGO

O n the whole, few species of shrews are truly threatened, having demonstrated their adaptability to a wide range of climates and habitats. They are unfussy feeders, most species breed rapidly and frequently, and they have been extremely successful in many parts of the world.

This has proved just as well, for, like so many wild creatures, the shrews' natural habitat is coming under increasing pressure from farmers and developers intent on transforming wild areas for agriculture or settlement. Shrews prefer habitats with plenty of vegetation cover, such as hedgerows, meadows, and grasslands; in Great Britain, these are precisely the areas under greatest threat. In areas of high agricultural activity, shrews have also been put at risk by the increased use of pesticides and fertilizers. Pesticides increase in concentration as they proceed farther up the food chain. Shrews may unwittingly eat earthworms and other invertebrates whose bodies contain large doses of accumulated pesticide toxins. Water shrews are particularly vulnerable to pollution in rivers and streams. Major pollutants include agricultural runoff (pesticides and fertilizers washed off fields and into rivers by the rain), sewage outflow, and heavy-metal and other factory waste material. Drainage, canalization, and

Solenodons (below) *were unknown to science until the early 19th century.*

Pat Morris/Ardea

James H. Carmichael/NHPA

THEN & NOW

This map shows the present distribution, as far as can be ascertained, of the Cuban and Hispaniolan solenodons.

CUBAN AND HISPANIOLAN SOLENODONS

The two remaining species of solenodon are found only on two Caribbean islands—Hispaniola and Cuba. They were once also found on the neighboring island of Puerto Rico, but probably died out there some time before 1930. Both species are officially classified as endangered and are restricted to remote areas of mountain forest.

Earlier this century, it was thought that the Cuban solenodon was already extinct. In fact, it survives in many parts of Cuba, albeit in perilously low numbers. The Hispaniolan solenodon is, however, in great danger of becoming extinct in Haiti, although it is still found in a few areas of the Dominican Republic.

general disruption of their homes is another serious problem. In Great Britain, watercress beds have long provided a favorite habitat for water shrews. Destruction of these beds, particularly in southern England, has severely depleted shrew numbers.

Despite the overall success of shrews, a number of species are classified as rare or endangered. These include *Blarina carolinensis shermani*, a rare shrew from Florida, which is threatened by habitat destruction; the Bornean musk shrew, *Suncus ater*; and *Crocidura odorata goliath* from Africa. On a

The forested banks of the Layol River, Dominican Republic, are home to the Hispaniolan solenodon.

worldwide scale, there is still too little known about these secretive creatures to judge their status exactly. Many other species may be endangered or already extinct, although new species are also being discovered regularly.

CENTURIES OF SUFFERING

The future for the solenodons looks very bleak indeed. They are probably extinct on the island of Puerto Rico; the surviving individuals on Cuba and Hispaniola are almost certainly set to follow them. The history of their devastation dates back four centuries, to the years when European settlers were first colonizing the newly discovered West Indies.

The voyage of Columbus in 1492 opened up the Caribbean to European interests. The Spanish settled first on Hispaniola, at Santo Domingo. From there, both Cortés and Pizarro made their notorious pioneering voyages to Mexico and Peru respectively. Cuba and Puerto Rico were next to suffer Spanish conquest; by the 1640s, the English, French, and Dutch had also established themselves in the area, and the first successful sugar plantations were set up for exploitation by European traders. The Spanish exterminated most of the native human population; they and other settlers also introduced fatal contagious diseases. Accordingly, slaves were imported from Africa in huge numbers to work the sugar crops.

THE SOLENODONS' MAIN ENEMIES TODAY ARE ALIEN SPECIES OUT OF REACH OF THE LAW: FERAL CATS AND DOGS

The burgeoning trade in slaves, sugar, and other commercial enterprises did for the West Indies' plants and animals what the Spanish and other intruders did for the hapless native Caribs. Vast expanses of forest and other natural habitats were obliterated to accommodate plantations and settlements, with correspondingly dire effects upon the native island wildlife, which until that time had existed in peaceful isolation from the American mainland. But as far as the wildlife is concerned, this systematic destruction pales into insignificance when set against the introduction of the small Indian mongoose, *Herpestes auropunctatus*, to Jamaica by a plantation owner in 1872.

A FATAL INTRODUCTION

As early as the mid-17th century, black rats were ruining the sugar crops on the West Indian plantations. Having disembarked from settlers' ships, the opportunistic rats thrived on the readily accessible crops. Various species were introduced in attempts

ENDANGERED SPECIES

James H. Carmichael/NHPA

SOLENODONS

Habitat destruction is one factor in the decline of the solenodons; their low reproductive rate also plays its part. But the main threat to their survival has been the introduction of predators and competitors. The two surviving species were not even seen by European eyes until the mid-1830s. Today, they are both on the verge of extinction.

Until a few years ago their status was believed to be even more critical; the tiny populations of both species seemed powerless against their enemies, notably feral cats and dogs. In 1974–1975, however, three solenodons were found in two areas of Oriente Province, eastern Cuba. A subsequent survey revealed that, while numbers were far from healthy, the solenodon was in fact more widespread than previously supposed. Apparently the local farmers had long been aware of this. They, however, had been taking no interest in the solenodons since the insectivores were not pests, could not be eaten, and possessed commercially worthless pelts.

Following the survey, however, a new danger arose. Locals and farmers in the

CONSERVATION MEASURES

● Although several protected preserves have been established for solenodons on their island homes, their best hope of survival seems to lie in captivity. Their future may well depend on how successful zoos are at keeping and breeding solenodons. So far, progress has been slow.

● Both species of solenodons are protected by law on their island homes of Cuba and Hispaniola. However, their main predators

vicinity of the animals started to set traps for them, hoping to achieve a few minutes of fame on television and in newspapers. So, ironically, the rare species had been safer while the world still believed them to be on the brink of extinction.

THE HISPANIOLAN SOLENODON—AN ANCIENT SPECIES DOOMED TO EXTINCTION?

Inset picture Pat Morris/Ardea

today—feral cats and dogs—are outside the law in that they have no owners to control them.

● Shrews face a far brighter future. In Great Britain, they are protected under the Wildlife and Countryside Act of 1981, which controls the killing or capture of many small mammals. It is now illegal to trap or kill shrews there without a special license. With or without the law, they seem set to thrive in their habitats in Europe.

SOLENODONS IN DANGER

THE CHART BELOW SHOWS HOW THE INTERNATIONAL UNION FOR THE CONSERVATION OF NATURE (IUCN), OR THE WORLD CONSERVATION UNION, CLASSIFIES THE TWO REMAINING SPECIES OF SOLENODONS. DESPITE LEGAL AND GOVERNMENTAL PROTECTION, THEIR NUMBERS CONTINUE TO DECREASE AS THEIR HABITAT IS DESTROYED AND THEY FALL PREY TO THE INTRODUCED THREAT OF CATS, DOGS, AND MONGOOSES.

CUBAN SOLENODON	ENDANGERED
HISPANIOLAN SOLENODON	ENDANGERED

ENDANGERED MEANS THAT THE ANIMAL IS IN DANGER OF EXTINCTION AND THAT ITS SURVIVAL IS UNLIKELY UNLESS STEPS ARE TAKEN TO SAVE IT.

Pat Morris/Ardea

to combat the rats through biological control; these included ferrets, ferocious ants, and giant toads. The first mongooses to arrive—just nine of them—had a marked effect on the rats within six months of their release. The delighted planters released mongooses throughout the island; rat populations slumped and sugar harvests improved considerably, but it soon became uncomfortably clear that this small mongoose killed and ate indiscriminately. Its prey on Jamaica included animals ranging from

MONGOOSES HAD BEEN INTRODUCED TO JAMAICA BEFORE 1872, BUT WITHOUT SUCCESS: THE CAPTIVE-BRED ANIMALS WERE REPORTED TO BE AFRAID OF RATS

prize livestock and pet kittens to ground-nesting birds and lizards. Furthermore, this irrepressible creature was stripping the plantations of avocados, pineapples, coconuts, bananas, and corn.

Nevertheless, the mongoose was introduced to other islands including Puerto Rico, Trinidad, Cuba, and Hispaniola. By the turn of the century, most island authorities in the West Indies had banned its importation, but the legislation arrived too late: The destruction had been set in motion. In 1918, an analysis was made of the stomach contents of nearly 200 mongooses from Trinidad. It was estimated that, over a three-month period, a single mongoose ate 26 rats, more than 500 grasshoppers, 14 birds, 17 lizards, 18 snakes, and 30 frogs or toads. The mongoose has almost single-handedly exterminated the Jamaican and St. Vincent rice rats, and the water vole, rice rat, and spiny pocket mouse on Trinidad. Its victims on Hispaniola, Puerto Rico, and Cuba include the ill-fated solenodons. The crowning blow came in 1950, when the mongoose was discovered to be a significant carrier of rabies. It

OUT OF ACTION

It is widely believed that shrews are extremely nervous and liable to die of shock if they hear a loud noise, such as a clap of thunder or a gunshot. Shrews are much tougher than this suggests, but if they are close to starvation, they are much more susceptible to death by any means.

There are several reports of shrews weakly tottering around, then dropping dead. Such sightings usually occur in the early morning. This phenomenon, known as cold starvation, results from a lack of food combined with particularly low air temperatures. It is a major cause of death among shrews.

Among shrews' natural predators are tawny and barn owls, kestrels and other birds of prey, weasels, stoats, polecats, and foxes. Many of these predators prefer to take small rodents rather than shrews if they are plentiful. Cats and dogs may catch shrews but do not usually eat them; they are often put off by the shrews' strong, musky smell. More shrews are preyed upon in summer and autumn, when there are plenty of young shrews around searching for food and establishing territories.

Other causes of death are old age and excessive tooth wear, leading to an inability to process sufficient food.

William Paton/NHPA

The small Indian mongoose (above) is one of several species introduced by humans to the West Indies that prey on solenodons.

ALONGSIDE MAN

THE FARMER'S FRIEND

In many places, shrews live in close proximity to humans. They are sometimes lumped in with rats and mice as pests or vermin, particularly in agricultural areas. They are, however, extremely helpful to farmers, because they are able to consume vast quantities of invertebrates that might otherwise harm farmers' crops. The European common and pygmy shrews, for example, eat crane flies and caterpillars; in parts of North America, shrews feed on the larvae of pine sawflies, which cause untold damage to conifer forests.

But shrews have suffered undeserved bad press since Roman times, giving rise to many superstitions. The Romans thought shrews brought bad luck. In the Middle Ages, it was believed that shrews caused lameness in horses and cattle. In truth, however, shrews are not as fierce as once supposed; if they bite or fight, it is only to defend their territories with their precious supplies of food.

is generally acknowledged, even today, that the small Indian mongoose in the Caribbean has wreaked more destruction upon wildlife than any other animal deliberately introduced by humans.

RECOVERY IMPOSSIBLE

Not all the blame for the solenodons' demise can be laid upon the Indian mongoose—or even on the shortsighted sugar traders who promoted its lethal introduction. The rats themselves preyed upon the insectivores and raided their food sources; cats and dogs, which were running feral soon after their introduction onto the islands, have come to be recognized as key predators on many species of native Caribbean wildlife. More recently, the solenodons have suffered further destruction of their habitat to provide much-needed living and farming space for the islands' surging populations.

Today, solenodons exist only in inaccessible mountain regions and in protected forest preserves established by the government in an effort to safeguard their future. Another factor in their decline is their low reproductive rate. Centuries ago, in the absence of predators—except for a few birds of prey and boa constrictors—this was probably sufficient. With the introduction of alien predators, however, the rate of predation often exceeds the birthrate and prevents the solenodon population from recovering. Today, the two remaining species are the most threatened of all insectivores and among the most endangered species on Earth. ∎

INTO THE FUTURE

Unless efforts are made to limit the destruction of the forest homes of the two remaining species of solenodons, they are probably doomed to extinction in the wild. The governments of Cuba and Haiti have made efforts to establish protected mountain preserves for the solenodons, but much more still needs to be done to safeguard their survival. Perhaps their best hope lies in captivity, in the captive-breeding programs that many zoos are now running to save rare species. Compared to many animals, however, relatively little is known about solenodons either in the wild or in captivity. Their rarity makes research difficult, as do their nocturnal habits and secretive natures.

Many species of shrews have also become extinct over the last few thousand years. These

PREDICTION

SITUATION DESPERATE

In direct contrast to most shrews, solenodons seem almost certain to die out in the wild unless extreme measures are taken to protect them from introduced predators in their few remaining mountain strongholds in the Caribbean.

include species that once inhabited various islands in the Mediterranean. They died out about 4,000–5,000 years ago, probably at the same time as the first human settlers arrived on the islands.

But people have also been responsible for successfully, if accidentally, introducing shrew species to new countries where they have quickly made themselves at home. One such example is the lesser white-toothed or Scilly shrew, which presumably reached the Scilly Isles as a stowaway onboard trading ships.

Despite their undeserved reputation as harbingers of evil and pests to agriculture, shrews suffer little persecution from man; we may even confess to a grudging admiration of the fearlessness and indomitability of these minuscule creatures. Provided that we allow them enough undisturbed pockets of land where they can find food and shelter, shrews seem set to thrive. ■

DISCOVERIES

Since the arrival of the Spanish in the 16th century, the solenodons have never been common, and for several decades they were believed extinct. Scientists were first able to describe the Cuban solenodon in 1833. By this time, it was already succumbing to predation, and for the rest of the 19th century it was considered extinct. In 1909, however, it was "rediscovered." The Hispaniolan species, too, was feared lost to the world until it reappeared in 1907.

New shrews are being discovered on a regular basis. In the early 1990s, a new type of shrew was discovered in Tanzania, Africa, by a group of German scientists. They named the shrew *Crocidura desperata*, to reflect the fact that its forest home was in danger of being destroyed and in increasing need of protection. The new shrew measures 3 in (7.6 cm) along its head and body and has thick, gray-brown fur. It was the latest of twenty new species of shrews discovered by this team of scientists in the last ten years.

Illustration Kim Thompson

SLOTHS

RELATIONS

The sloths are members of the Edentata, or "toothless" order, of mammals, which also includes:

GIANT ANTEATER

SILKY ANTEATER

TAMANDUAS

GIANT ARMADILLO

HAIRY ARMADILLOS

SIX-BANDED ARMADILLO

John Lythgoe/Planet Earth Pictures

SLOW AND STEADY

SLOTHS SPEND WHOLE DAYS SEEMINGLY INACTIVE, AND WHEN THEY DO MOVE IT IS AT A PAINFULLY SLOW PACE. BUT THIS IS NOT LAZINESS; IT IS A SUPERBLY EFFECTIVE STRATEGY FOR CONSERVING ENERGY

U sed as a term of mild derision, the word *sloth* inspires images of laziness and inactivity. This unflattering image also applies to the mammal of the same name of the tropical forests of Central and South America. But the sloth's very "slothfulness" is one of the reasons behind its success at a time when many large forest animals are in rapid and terminal decline. Its behavior has evolved over a long period of time to suit a finely balanced forest existence.

Today, five species of sloths can be found in the American tropics. They are so numerous in some areas that they comprise up to 25 percent of the mammal biomass—the total mass of all living mammals in the rain forest. This is not to suggest that sloths are too successful: They are very much at the whim of human activities. As a result of deforestation, coupled with road deaths along new routes through forest areas and a background of hunting and persecution, the fate of the sloth hangs in the balance.

CLASSIFICATION

Sloths are members of the Edentata order, or so-called "toothless" animals, together with the anteaters and armadillos. These are often grouped with the pangolins, order Pholidota.

ORDER

Edentata

FAMILY

Bradypodidae

GENUS

Bradypus
(three-toed sloths)

SPECIES

B. tridactylus
(pale-throated sloth)

B. variegatus
(brown-throated sloth)

B. torquatus
(maned sloth)

FAMILY

Megalonychidae
(two-toed sloths)

GENUS

Choloepus
(two-toed sloths)

SPECIES

C. didactylus
(Linne's sloth)

C. hoffmanni
(Hoffmann's sloth)

The two distinct genera of sloths can most easily be distinguished by the numbers of fingers they possess; sloths of the genus *Choloepus* have two fingers, or "toes," while those of the genus *Bradypus* have three. There are other differences as well—the nostrils of two-toed sloths are larger and farther apart, and their eyes are more prominent. Their small ears are almost invisible, the distinctly shorter neck is less mobile, and the tail is smaller than in three-toed sloths. Two-toed sloths are less specialist feeders than three-toed sloths, and consequently they move more actively from tree to tree in search of food items.

LIVING HAMMOCKS

Sloths have become highly specialized to their forest environment—in their body structure, consumption of food energy, and breeding strategies. They eat, sleep, mate, and give birth in what to humans would seem to be a most uncomfortable upside-down position. Long forelimbs used as tension rods suspend the body from branches and are coupled with fingers that support hooked claws for a firm grip. The upside-down habit has also resulted in a short pelvis and an increased number of neck bones compared with most mammals; consequently, three-toed sloths can rotate their heads about 270 degrees. Conveniently,

The sleepy gaze of Hoffmann's sloth (above) *speaks volumes about its super-relaxed lifestyle.*

Rod Williams/Bruce Coleman Ltd.

Michael Fogden/Oxford Scientific Films

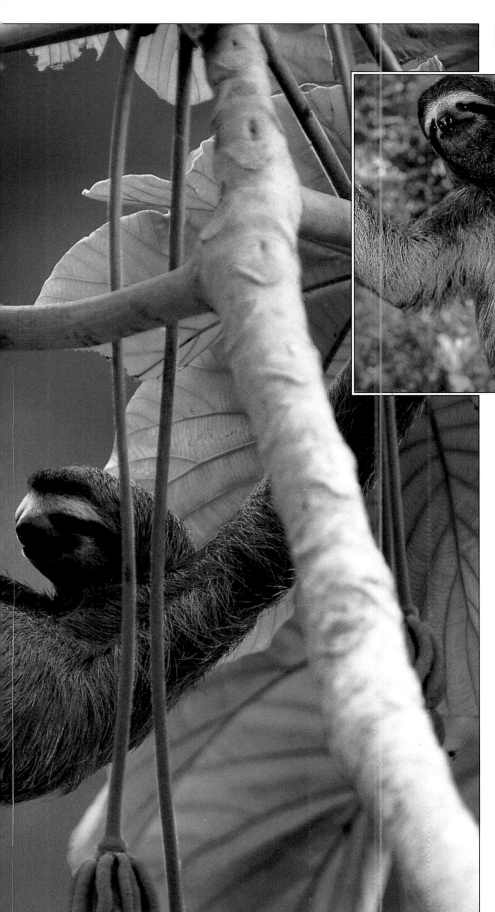

Norbert Wu/Planet Earth Pictures

FINGERS AND TOES

The two genera of sloths can easily be distinguished by the number of fingers they possess; the two species of the genus *Choloepus* have two fingers, while those of the genus *Bradypus* have three. Both genera have three toes.

In spite of this fact, the two-fingered forms are called two-toed sloths, whereas the three-fingered forms are called three-toed sloths.

On all species, the fingers are closely united and each has a sharp, hooked claw sheathing the extreme joint.

several of the vital organs have rotated to fit in with the animal's most frequent upside-down position. For example, the liver has rotated to the right, about 135 degrees in the direction of the back, and is completely covered by the displaced stomach, so that it does not touch the abdominal wall. The spleen and the pancreas have also shifted by a similar amount, and are not located on the left as in other mammals, but on the right, near the exit to the stomach.

NOT ENTIRELY TOOTHLESS

Sloths, along with anteaters and armadillos, belong to the Edentata (EE-den-TAH-tah) order. This word means "without teeth" but is in fact a misnomer, since

Suspended animation: Even in her sleep, this three-toed sloth is firmly hooked to her home tree.

only the anteaters wholly lack teeth; sloths and armadillos have simple, rootless molars, which grow throughout the animal's life. Because sloths exist mostly on a diet of leaves gathered from the canopy of the rain forest, their teeth are used to grind vegetation to a size that can be conveniently swallowed.

The origin of the edentates is not fully known. Most experts agree, however, that sixty million years ago, at the dawn of the mammal age, edentates had already diverged into small, armorless animals—which rapidly became extinct—and the *Xenarthra* (zen-ARTH-rah) from which living edentates are descended. The variations seen in edentates today were also found in some of the ancient xenarthrans.

Two vegetarian groups of xenarthrans died out— the *Glyptodonts* (huge armadillo-like creatures) and the ground sloths, including *Megatherium*, which weighed three tons and were up to ten times larger than today's sloths. Unable to drag themselves up into the trees, these mammoth beasts lumbered around on the ground. They reared up on two legs, supported by a sturdy tail, to browse on the leafy tree canopy, hooking down branches with their three-clawed forefeet.

These bulky ancestors neither looked nor behaved like their modern descendants. They were isolated on their island home of South America, sixty-five million years ago, and had as competition nothing more dangerous than early marsupials and other primitive mammals. Consequently the sloths were lords of the land. They even managed to reach southern North America and the West Indies at the height of their abundance, thirty million years ago, having apparently rafted across the sea and arrived as immigrants. However, as advanced and highly adaptable mammalian invaders from the north entered edentate domain, these huge and clumsy edentates were outcompeted, their only survivors being the species that had relatively specialized lifestyles, such as the anteaters, armadillos, and tree-dwelling sloths. ∎

THE SLOTHS' FAMILY TREE

The edentates are an unusual collection of animals and include some of the most bizarre mammals on earth. There are four families, thirteen genera, and twenty-nine species of living edentates, which originated from the Xenarthra some sixty million years ago. All edentates can be distinguished from all other mammals by the special supporting bones between their vertebrae.

HOFFMANN'S TWO-TOED SLOTH
Choloepus hoffmanni (co-LEE-pus hoff-MAN-ee)

Smaller than its two-toed cousin, Hoffmann's sloth lives in both Central and South America. Curiously, there seem to be far more females than males in the wild.

LINNE'S TWO-TOED SLOTH
Choloepus didactylus (co-LEE-pus die-dak-TIE-lus)

Also known as the unau, Linne's sloth has a wide distribution across northern South America, including the Amazon Basin. It is still fairly numerous.

ANCESTORS

MEGATHERIUM
This giant ground sloth was abundant in North and South America. At 20 ft (6 m) long and weighing over three tons, *Megatherium* was as big as a small elephant. It is thought to have been a browsing or grazing species of grassy woodlands or wooded plains. It walked on the sides of its hind feet and on the knuckles of its forefeet, as anteaters do today.

Color illustrations Kim Thompson

B/W illustrations Ruth Grewcock

BROWN-THROATED THREE-TOED SLOTH

Bradypus variegatus
(*BRAD-ee-pus varri-eh-GAHT-us*)

This species can be found from Guatemala south to northern Argentina. Unlike the nocturnal two-toed sloths, it is apparently active by day as well as by night.

PALE-THROATED THREE-TOED SLOTH

Bradypus tridactylus
(*BRAD-ee-pus try-dak-TIE-luss*)

This is the most common of the three-toed sloths, although limited in range. It is also known as the ai, due to the sound of its distinctive mating call.

MANED SLOTH

Bradypus torquatus
(*BRAD-ee-pus tor-CAHT-us*)

This extremely rare species is found only in the Atlantic coastal forests of eastern Brazil. It is named after the long, dark hairs growing on its forequarters.

THREE-TOED SLOTHS

TWO-TOED SLOTHS

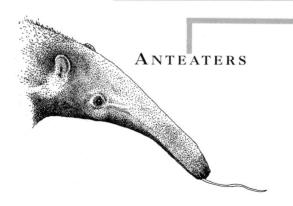

ANTEATERS

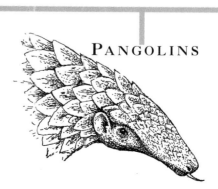

PANGOLINS

ARMADILLOS

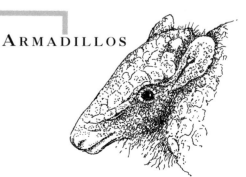

ALL EDENTATES

ANATOMY:
THE THREE-TOED SLOTH

Sloths differ little in overall size. Two-toed sloths (above right) reach a head-and-body length of 23–28 in (58–71 cm); three-toed sloths are slightly smaller, growing to a head-and-body length of 22–24 in (56–61 cm).

THREE-TOED SLOTH

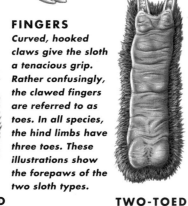

FINGERS
Curved, hooked claws give the sloth a tenacious grip. Rather confusingly, the clawed fingers are referred to as toes. In all species, the hind limbs have three toes. These illustrations show the forepaws of the two sloth types.

THREE-TOED SLOTH

TWO-TOED SLOTH

THE FACE
is nearly naked, with a rigid expression. The facial muscles are much reduced except for those used for chewing. Hard, horny lips help in grasping leaves.

THE EYES
are small and directed forward. They apparently give the sloth color vision.

THE COAT
has two layers. The underfur is short and fine, while the overcoat consists of longer and coarser hairs. The green hue of the fur results from the color of two species of blue-green algae that grow along grooves in the hair shafts. The long hair of the overcoat is an adaptation to conserve body heat.

X
R A Y

SLOTH SKELETON
The skeleton of the sloth reflects its exclusively arboreal lifestyle, with the skeleton used to support the hanging body weight. The limbs are long and used as tension rods rather than pillars of support, as is usual in most other mammals. As in other edentates, the vertebrae are reinforced by bony structures called xenarthrales, which give support to the back.

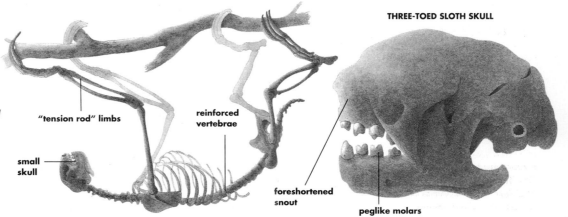

THREE-TOED SLOTH SKULL

"tension rod" limbs

reinforced vertebrae

small skull

foreshortened snout

peglike molars

X-ray illustrations Elisabeth Smith

THE FORELIMBS

are longer than the hind limbs, particularly in three-toed sloths.

FUR

The sloth's coat looks shaggy and moth eaten. In fact, it is often full of tiny moths. The green tinge derives from algae that find the damp, warm fur ideal; they also provide camouflage.

CLASSIFICATION

GENUS: *BRADYPUS*

SPECIES: *TRIDACTYLUS*

SIZE

HEAD–BODY LENGTH: 16–24 IN (40–60 CM)

TAIL LENGTH: 0.8–3.5 IN (2–9 CM)

WEIGHT: 5–12 LB (2.2–5.5 KG)

WEIGHT AT BIRTH: 7–8.8 OZ (200–250 G)

COLORATION

GENERALLY GRAY-BROWN, SLIGHTLY DARKER ON THE HEAD AND FACE. ON THE SHOULDERS THERE IS USUALLY A PALE AREA WITH BROWN MARKINGS. OFTEN THE COAT COLOR APPEARS GREEN, DUE TO THE ALGAE GROWING IN THE FUR. THERE IS CONSIDERABLE VARIATION IN COAT COLOR AMONG SOME INDIVIDUALS OF CERTAIN SPECIES

FEATURES

CURVED CLAWS

ROUNDED HEAD WITH FLATTENED FACE

THREE DIGITS ON EACH FOREFOOT AND HIND FOOT

LONG ARMS

STUMPY TAIL

SMALL EYES

SMALL, INCONSPICUOUS EARS

COARSE, SHAGGY FUR COAT

THE TAIL

is short and stumpy and looks rather an afterthought. It is in fact redundant, since the sloth does not need to balance while moving through the trees.

SLOTH SKULLS

The three-toed sloth's skull is block shaped with a flattened snout, whereas the two-toed sloth has a slightly more elongated skull. In both genera the zygomatic arch (a cheekbone) is not complete. There are no canine or incisor teeth; the simple, peglike cheek teeth grow throughout the animal's life. They have high cusps and form efficient surfaces for grinding down leaves.

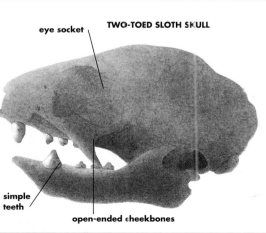

eye socket   TWO-TOED SLOTH SKULL

simple teeth

open-ended cheekbones

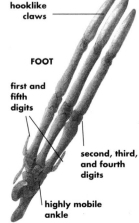

hooklike claws

FOOT

first and fifth digits

second, third, and fourth digits

highly mobile ankle

HANDS AND FEET

The hooklike hands and feet are specially adapted to an arboreal life. In the foot (left), the first and fifth digits barely exist. The central digits are mostly bound within the foot, and the claws are reinforced within by a toe bone. The outer digits of the hand (below) are also reduced. With tendons in the rest position (shown) the claw makes an angle of 90° with the hand.

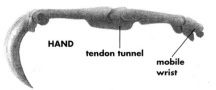

HAND

tendon tunnel

mobile wrist

Main illustration Steve Kingston

HANGING AROUND

IN A SLOTH'S VIEW OF THE WORLD, THE GROUND TOWERS OVER ITS HEAD AND THE SKY STRETCHES AWAY FROM THE TREES BENEATH ITS FEET—FOR IT IS ONLY FULLY RELAXED WHEN WHOLLY UPSIDE DOWN

Sloths live in a complex habitat in terms of both the great diversity of tree species present and also the structural complexity of the vegetation.

The crowns of forest trees are often thick with liana vines, and the interlocking tree canopy provides a network of routes and footholds for the sloth's long, hooked feet. The last joints of the toe digits are in fact the "hooks"; they can grip like a vise even while the wrist is rotated. The limb joints are loosely enclosed, and most have smoothly articulated bones that allow supple and fluid movement.

> THE ABILITY TO SWIM BENEFITS SLOTHS GREATLY: THEY HAVE BEEN KNOWN TO SLIP ACCIDENTALLY FROM RIVERSIDE TRUMPET TREES WHILE FEEDING

The hooklike claws hinge in one plane only—like a penknife blade—but the sloth can actually rotate its feet through almost 180 degrees and make use of slender supports. It is therefore better adapted to moving along thin lianas than heavy branches. A tree that supports a healthy growth of lianas will often also harbor sloths.

TROUBLE DOWN BELOW

If it has to, a sloth will cross the forest floor to move from one tree to another—but it is vulnerable to alert predators such as jaguars, ocelots, and other cats, and movement along the ground necessitates a slow crawl on the feet and forearms. This form of locomotion is clearly alien to a sloth, because it must grovel along with its belly dragging over the ground. If attacked on the ground, it lashes out at the predator with its sharp claws, often inflicting deep lacerations. It can also bite hard. Even so, a sloth caught down on the ground provides an easily sub-

dued and substantial meal, particularly for a prowling feline. The physical effort involved in ground travel is so great that the sloth must rest as soon as it regains the safety of the trees.

Sloths can swim well; they have even been known to cross the Amazon River itself, although the feat may take them a few hours. This swimming ability is one reason why sloths are so widely distributed through the often-flooded Amazon forests.

Three-toed sloths are active, at least sporadically, for more than ten hours during any given day, whereas two-toed sloths are only active for, on average, seven and a half hours during the same time period. The daily activity pattern between the two species also varies; the three-toed species are active during both the day and the night, whereas the two-toed species are strictly nocturnal. This may help to explain why the pale-throated three-toed sloth is so

Sloths are surprisingly proficient swimmers; they use a modified breaststroke action (above).

Sloths spend almost their entire lives in the tree canopy, clinging tightly to a trunk or bough.

familiar to humans and has been so thoroughly studied, although it has a considerably smaller range than some of its less-familiar relatives.

Hoffmann's two-toed sloth tends to change trees more frequently and travel greater daily distances than the brown-throated three-toed sloth. Since the latter spends longer periods of time in one tree, feeding is confined to this tree species and other plant species supported by it for longer periods of time. Therefore, the brown-throated sloth is a more specialized feeder than its two-toed relative and relies heavily on the young leaves, twigs, and buds of the cecropia, or trumpet tree. Two-toed sloths, although larger, have a wider choice of food items due to their increased mobility.

ELEVEN TO ONE

Field research has revealed that Hoffmann's two-toed sloth exists in ratios of eleven females to one male. No one knows why this sex ratio should be so off-kilter, but it certainly makes sense to have such a high ratio of females to males to ensure continued survival in a species that has an unusually long gestation period (almost one year). One problem with this particular study, however, is that female Hoffmann's sloths tend to gather in groups, whereas the males are loners. As such, it would have been easy to overlook males in forest surveys, and this ratio may not represent the actual ratio. ∎

DAILY ACTIVITY

Sloths have a good sense of smell, a poorly defined sense of hearing, and the use of color vision, which helps them as they move around the forest. They spend most of their time—up to sixteen hours per day—sleeping or resting, and the remainder of their time feeding. Sloths have a highly variable body temperature, so when it is at rest, it will try to pull itself into a compact, hanging-basket shape by drawing all its feet close together on its perch in the tree canopy. The feet radiate heat, so it is in the sloth's interest to bunch them together and retain energy. Similarly, when resting in a tree fork, a sloth will form a ball shape and tuck its head on its chest, again reducing its body size and hence heat loss.

HABITATS

Sloths have precise habitat needs. They live only in dense forests that provide them with a constant supply of leaves, and the forest must be large enough to support a viable breeding population of sloths. Trees need to be large enough and close enough together to enable sloths to move around the forest at canopy height as and when necessary. In fact, the status of sloth species parallels the status of the neotropical deciduous forests and rain forests.

HABITAT PREFERENCES

Of the two-toed species, Linne's sloth is common and widespread in northern South America as far south as the Amazon Basin, whereas the generally smaller Hoffmann's sloth is less well known, although it has a wider range from Nicaragua to Peru and Central Brazil. The pale-throated three-toed sloth ranges from Central America to northern Argentina; it is the most common and familiar species. The brown-throated sloth has an enormous range, extending from Guatemala and Honduras to northern Argentina. The maned sloth is confined to eastern Brazil.

Despite widespread deforestation, forest cover still cloaks much of Central and South America, and sloths are still relatively common in many forest areas. The types of forest preferred vary among species: Studies in Venezuela have shown that pale-throated and brown-throated three-toed sloths occur mainly in evergreen forest, but also inhabit deciduous forest and scattered trees in woodland pasture

A female pale-throated sloth launches herself elegantly, if cautiously, toward some tasty foliage (right). Her youngster merely clings more tightly, sinking its tiny claws into her thick belly fur.

Luiz Claudio Marigo/Bruce Coleman Ltd.

areas. Although representatives of both two- and three-toed sloths coincide in tropical forests across much of their range, different species within the same genus occupy more or less exclusive geographical ranges. These closely related species differ little in body weight and have such similar lifestyles that it appears that they are unable to coexist.

Where two-toed and three-toed sloths occur within the same area of forest, the two-toed form is usually at least 25 percent heavier than its relative and the two species exploit the forest's resources in different ways. Body size does seem to affect the distribution and activity patterns of the two major types of sloths. Whereas the larger two-toed sloths can survive in tropical mountain slopes and range into cloud forest, the three-toed sloths are confined to lower elevations. This greater requirement for energy is thought to be the reason for the three-toed sloth's round-the-clock activities. In São Paulo Botanical Gardens, down south in the subtropical parts of its range, the pale-throated three-toed sloth can survive temperatures below freezing.

As might be expected, sloths do not often cover great distances within the forest; individuals may

DISTRIBUTION

All sloths are confined to the tropical forests of Central and South America. They cannot live in more open habitats because they rely on a dense tree canopy. They are not found in more temperate zones because they are unable to regulate their body temperature.

KEY

PALE-THROATED SLOTH

BROWN-THROATED SLOTH

MANED SLOTH

HOFFMANN'S SLOTH

LINNE'S SLOTH

stay put in the same tree for several nights. There is, however, some evidence of limited migration in the pale-throated three-toed sloth. In Guyana, a male of this species was recorded as having moved five miles (8 km) over a forty-eight-day period during the rainy season (May–June). If this rate of movement does not seem remarkable, it should perhaps be remembered that it is unusual for a sloth to move far at all—only one in ten pale-throated three-toed sloths move more than 125 ft (38 m) in a day.

ENEMIES

The slow sloth regularly provides a sought-after meal for predators. Three of its greatest enemies are the jaguar, the ocelot, and the world's largest species of eagle, the harpy. Although jaguars occur in savanna and semidesert areas, they are among the

---

A SIGNIFICANT NUMBER OF SLOTHS FALL TO FELINE PREDATORS, DESPITE THEIR SUPERB NATURAL CAMOUFLAGE

---

top predators within the tropical forests. They will eat peccaries, capybaras, and tapirs in addition to sloths, and are solitary, powerful hunters.

The ocelot is a much smaller species of cat, but like the jaguar it occurs in a wide range of habitats from semiarid deserts to tropical forests. It relies on its stunningly beautiful spotted coat to conceal it among the dappled, shady forest foliage while it

KEEPING WARM IN THE TROPICS

Like armadillos and anteaters, sloths have very low but variable body temperatures—in their case around 86–93.2°F (30–34°C) in waking hours. A sloth cools off during the early morning, on days of wet weather, or when otherwise inactive. This helps it to conserve energy—sloths turn food into energy less than half as fast as would be expected for a creature of their size. Their skeletal muscles are reduced, weighing only 25 percent of a typical animal's body weight, compared with 45 percent in most other mammal species. This lack of heat-producing muscle is part of the reason why sloths cannot control their body temperature.

When cool, a sloth cannot shiver to warm up, so it regulates its temperature by inhabiting trees with exposed crowns. In this way, it can warm up or cool down by moving into or out of sunlight. Out in the sunshine, a sloth's body temperature will rapidly rise to the ambient temperature within a couple of hours. At dawn, sloths can be seen hanging from the peaks of tree crowns, facing east, basking in the early rays of the sun. In some areas, locals refer to the three-toed sloth as the "sun sloth." This is due to its sunbathing activities, and also because this species exposes a brilliant orange-red patch of fine fur along its back when sunning itself.

ZEFA

stalks unwitting prey such as sleeping sloths. Both of these cat species suffer from persecution and the loss of their natural habitats.

The harpy eagle is a major predator on sloths. Three-toed sloths are particularly vulnerable to predation by this giant eagle early in the day when they are sitting on the sunlit side of the tree canopy sunning themselves. Sloth remains have also been found in the stomachs of an anaconda and a coati (a member of the raccoon family), although the coati probably scavenged the sloth as carrion. The remains of an immature sloth have been found in the stomach of a margay; in this instance, the cat's forehead had been badly slashed, possibly by the young sloth's mother.

ALGAE TO THE RESCUE

It is not surprising that sloths have so many enemies; to escape trouble, their top speed is a dismal 1.2 mph (1.9 km/h), and the 100-yard dash would take about twenty-two minutes. But sloths are not entirely defenseless: In addition to lashing out with tooth and claw, they can make use of the humid forest conditions to provide camouflage. Primitive algae thrive in such wet conditions, and the sloth's thick, matted body hair has evolved to nurture such algal growths. Two species of blue-green algae flourish in special

MPL Fogden/Bruce Coleman Ltd.

FOCUS ON

BARRO COLORADO ISLAND

The tiny Barro Colorado Island lies in the artificially created Gatun Sea, close to the northern coast of Panama. The Panama Canal, which splits the country from north to south, flows through the Gatun Sea. The island was created by the rising of the waters at the beginning of the century, resulting from the excavation of the Panama Canal. It has been protected as a biological research station since soon after its newfound isolation.

The island supports tropical forest, with many species found there that mirror those found on the Panamanian mainland. But this microhabitat lacks many of the predatory cats and eagles, so prey species such as sloths, peccaries, and coatis have thrived tremendously. The island is popular with bird-watchers, and several bird species are more easily observed on the island than elsewhere. These include the crested guan, great tinamou, white-whiskered puffbird, and barred woodcreeper.

As a sloth haven, Barro Colorado is ideal, but it is not a truly natural preserve area. It is too small to support viable breeding populations of, for example, solitary big cats, which typically occur at lower densities than their prey species. On small islands, such species eventually outstrip their food supply.

TEMPERATURE AND RAINFALL

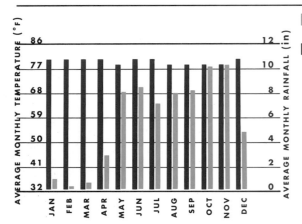

■ RAINFALL

■ TEMPERATURE

Panama's Caribbean (northeast) coast is far wetter than the Pacific (southwest) coast, because the northeasterly trade winds shed their rain as they reach land. This climatic pattern is consistent even in the narrowest parts of Panama.

grooves running along the hairs. The growth of these primitive plants on the sloth gives the fur a greenish tinge, which is particularly noticeable during the wet season—the time of year when the algae grow most profusely. In addition to adding a greenish hue to the sloth's fur, this algae provides a source of food for three species of small pyralid moths which also live within the sloth's shaggy coat. Huddled up and suspended from a branch, the moldering green sloth resembles a bunch of old leaves and is invisible to its would-be predators. ■

NEIGHBORS

The jaguar-free Barro Colorado is ideal for ground-nesting birds such as the tinamou and guan, although the locally abundant coatis and peccaries tend to rob them of their eggs.

GREAT TINAMOU

This elusive gamebird is far more often heard than seen. It prefers humid lowland forests.

CRESTED GUAN

The guan's overall range and numbers are declining due to deforestation and hunting pressure.

Neighbors: great tinamou Sean Milne, all others Craig Robson/Wildlife Art Agency

BARRO COLORADO

The island covers an area of about 5.8 sq mi (15 sq km) and lies northwest of the Panama Canal in the Gatun Sea. Panama itself forms a narrow isthmus between Costa Rica in Central America and Colombia in South America; the Gatun Sea lies roughly halfway along the Panama mainland.

Panama Canal

PANAMA

Pacific Ocean

■ **BARRO COLORADO ISLAND**

COLLARED PECCARY

This small, abundant, and social pig lives in a wide range of habitats, from dry deserts to tropical forests.

PUFFBIRD

Puffbirds have prominent "mustache" tufts. They feed on large insects, frogs, and small lizards in the forests.

BOA CONSTRICTOR

Boas grow to 11 ft (3.4 m) long and can kill mammals as large as young peccaries and deer.

MORPHO BUTTERFLY

These bright blue butterflies drift over the forest canopy, the males flying high to attract the females.

WOODCREEPER

Using its curved bill, the barred woodcreeper probes crevices in tree bark for its insect prey.

FOOD AND FEEDING

The sloth's monotonous diet of leaves is a low-energy source of food—the calories are bound up in cellulose, which is hard to break down even in the sloth's large, multichambered stomach. This constant diet of leaves, which are high in levels of alkaloids and tannins, stains the sloth's cheek teeth a rich brown color.

Whereas two-toed sloths are thought to feed on the leaves of several types of trees, three-toed sloths are probably more restricted in their diet, preferring the leaves of the trumpet tree. However, there have been instances where three-toed sloths have been released into forested habitat, for example into the park of the Muséu Paraense in Brazil, and have not limited themselves to leaves from the trumpet tree. In this instance they ate leaves from many other Amazonian trees from the orders Euphorbiaceae, Leguminosae, and Bombacaceae, even though trumpet trees were also abundant within the park.

A SLOTHFUL METABOLISM

The sloth has desperately slow metabolic processes. The weight of the stomach with its contents of chewed leaves has been found to make up 20–25 percent of a sloth's total body weight. This sludgy burden may remain in the stomach for up to a month before passing on to the small intestine. The leaf diet is high in fiber, and the slow rate of digestion does not produce the high body temperature necessary to sustain a typical mammal. To compensate, the sloth's body temperature fluctuates, rising during the day when the creature is actively foraging and declining during the night when the animal is sleeping and digestion is taking place. At night the sloth's body temperature may fall to around 68°F (20°C), similar to the ambient forest temperature.

DINING ALOFT

The three-toed sloth is often seen eating in the trumpet tree, which proliferates beside forest streams (right). It nestles securely in the branches and reaches out to hook in leafy boughs and rip off foliage, passing it slowly to the mouth.

SIGHT

THE SLOTH'S STOMACH

A sloth's stomach is relatively large and complex, occupying up to one-third of the body, and is divided into several different chambers. Similar in many ways to a cow's stomach, it is most unlike the simple stomachs of the insectivorous members of the edentates, such as anteaters and armadillos.

This enlarged stomach is in keeping with the sloth's exclusive diet of leaves. The left half of the stomach has thick, horny membranes that form three partially connected chambers. The largest of these is attached to the esophagus (gullet) and acts as a fermentation chamber, containing stomach juices that decompose leaves. The right half of the stomach is divided into two chambers linked by a narrow tunnel. One of these chambers has many glands and produces gastric juices to break down the leaves even further; it is referred to as the pepsin stomach. The second chamber has a strong muscular wall, and the two sections can be closed off from each other. The stomach also has several ceca (blind chambers) extending from it. The relative importance of all these sections and the precise workings of the stomach have still to be fully studied.

Color illustration Peter David Scott/Wildlife Art Agency

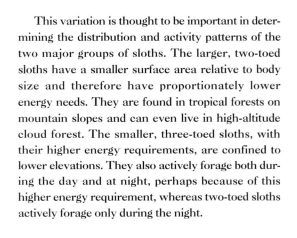

This variation is thought to be important in determining the distribution and activity patterns of the two major groups of sloths. The larger, two-toed sloths have a smaller surface area relative to body size and therefore have proportionately lower energy needs. They are found in tropical forests on mountain slopes and can even live in high-altitude cloud forest. The smaller, three-toed sloths, with their higher energy requirements, are confined to lower elevations. They also actively forage both during the day and at night, perhaps because of this higher energy requirement, whereas two-toed sloths actively forage only during the night.

SLOW TO GO

In keeping with their indolent image, sloths only pass urine and feces once a week, and laboriously descend to the forest floor to defecate at the base of a preferred tree. Descending from the forest canopy to the floor requires only a few minutes of the sloth's time each week and again acts as an energy conservation measure. On the forest floor, the sloth uses its short stump of a tail to scrape out a small hollow to use as a latrine.

The claws are not only essential for canopy travel, they make excellent hooks for food (right). Sloths are said to be messy eaters, however, dropping a fair amount of the foliage they tear off.

François Gohier/Ardea

Hoffmann's sloth changes trees more frequently and travels farther each day than the brown-throated sloth. As the latter species spends long periods of time in one tree, feeding is confined to this tree species for longer periods of time. Therefore, the brown-throated sloth is a more specialized feeder than its two-toed relative and relies heavily on the young leaves, tender twigs, and buds of the trumpet tree. Two-toed sloths have a wider choice of food items due to their increased mobility. ■

A three-toed sloth absorbed in the ritual of eating (right). *It also takes its time over digesting its meal.*

THE CECROPIA

The cecropia, or trumpet tree, is a member of the nettle family. It has hollow stems, which in some species are inhabited by biting ants of the genus *Azteca*. These ants rush out and attack any intruder that disturbs the plant and provide particularly good protection against destructive leaf-cutting ants. As well as giving the ants living space, the tree also provides nutrients for the ants on the leaf stalks. This mutually beneficial relationship is an excellent example of symbiosis.

In some species of trumpet tree these ants are absent, but the tree protects itself from leaf-cutting ants by a thick coating of wax on the stem, which prevents the ants from climbing.

A popular myth is that sloths feed only on trumpet trees. This is probably because trumpet trees are found in large numbers as colonists of riverbanks, forest edges, and clearings. Consequently, sloths along such exposed sites have a better chance of being seen by observers than animals in denser parts of the forest.

ON THE MOVE

Two-toed sloths have a broader diet than their three-toed cousins; in keeping with this, they are more mobile, changing trees to suit their feeding whims (left). They eat leaves and buds, as well as twigs, blossoms, fruit, and even root tubers and small prey.

Sylvestris/Frank Lane Picture Agency

DUNG

The regular use of one specific latrine acts as a powerful territorial message to other sloths in the area—but it also attracts several species of dung-eating insects. In one forest study in Brazil, nine species of beetles and moths were associated with sloth dung. Scavenging insects like herbivore dung because it is rich in nutrients; carnivore dung, by contrast, is made up mainly of hair and bone fragments. As an added bonus, the sloth will have already broken down and neutralized many of the toxic chemicals found in the leaves.

This rather unexpected role of the sloth is further evidence of its importance in the forest ecosystem. Sloths are thought to crop no less than 2 percent of a rain forest's total tree-leaf production. The further dependence on dung by such a range of invertebrates, which break it down and help the flow of nutrients back to the forest soils, is an essential part of forest life.

Illustration Peter David Scott/Wildlife Art Agency

TERRITORY

The use of territories by sloths is one of the little-known aspects of their lives that scientists are slowly beginning to unravel. It is quite clear, however, that they are not built for lively interaction with one another. Indeed, their very survival in the face of deadly predators depends for the most part on their solitude, which enables them to mimic a gently swaying bough of greenery. Social groups of sloths would be sitting ducks, and would probably invite a jaguar to commit mass slaughter.

Sloths have been intensively radio tracked on Barro Colorado Island, Panama, where there is a thriving sloth population in an accessible forest area. The home range of the three-toed sloth is usually less than 5 acres (2 ha), with a population density of less than 3 individuals per acre. Breeding seems to be an irregular event, and territorial or straightforward interaction is rarely recorded. On one occasion two sloths were observed fighting,

> SUBTLE VARIATIONS DEVELOP BETWEEN SLOTHS IN THEIR PREFERENCE FOR TREE TYPES: THIS HELPS REDUCE COMPETITION

apparently for possession of a trumpet tree; on another, two male three-toed sloths were heard hissing at each other and fell 30 ft (9 m) to the ground from a palm tree. Although obviously stunned by the fall, the animals retained their grip on each other with their hind feet after they landed on the ground. It took fully thirty seconds for them to disentangle themselves and begin to climb back up the liana vines toward the canopy. This encounter was taken to be a territorial dispute.

Patterns of communication between individuals are also poorly documented. Males are thought to advertise their presence to potential mates by wiping secretions from an anal gland onto the branches. In addition to this, the regular dung drops act as places for sloths to meet potential mates. Most sloths produce dull whistling noises, although the three-toed sloth gives a shrill, nasal "ai-ai" whistle—hence the local name of *ai* for this species—and the two-toed sloth hisses if disturbed.

FAVORITE TREES

Within a tropical forest, sloths will generally have a wide selection of tree species available to them to use. However, in general they tend to use trees that occur in the forest at medium to high densities. Rare trees are in general avoided. In studies

M. P. L. Fogden/Bruce Coleman Ltd.

on Barro Colorado Island, both two-toed and three-toed sloths were found to favor trees with large crowns that were regularly exposed to sunlight, and also trees that had a healthy growth of lianas within the tree canopy. Three-toed sloths chose trees more for the amount of time the crown of the tree was exposed to the sun, whereas two-toed sloths seemed to prefer trees with abundant lianas among the canopy. About one-fifth of all trees used by sloths were used by both three-toed and two-toed sloths.

The preference of three-toed sloths for sunny tree crowns results from the animals' movement through the forest canopy into and out of direct sunlight as their body temperatures change. It is thought that three-toed sloths risk starvation if there are several days in a row where there is little or no sunlight at midday, particularly if these conditions follow a rainy morning. The overall rate at which food passes through the sloth's gut is thought to depend, at least partly, upon the sloth's body temperature. This in turn depends partly upon the animal's exposure to sunlight. If a sloth is unable to warm up

On the off chance that an intruder manages to spot a sloth, or simply to stumble upon one, the surprised animal is likely to hiss and gape its mouth in threat (above).

B/W illustration Ruth Grewcock

KEEP OUT!
*Sloths can be fierce
in territorial defense.
This three-toed sloth
(below right) is
lashing out at a
two-toed trespasser.
The claws can inflict
painful wounds.*

Color illustration Robin Boutell/Wildlife Art Agency

in SIGHT

OUT OF ITS TREE

The sloth occasionally heads for the ground to move between trees where the canopy is too thin and also to defecate. It is not adept at moving along the ground and provides an incongruous sight—belly dragging along the floor, and forelimbs and hind limbs splayed at all angles. It crawls slowly along, hauling itself forward using the curved claws of the hand, which are either dug into the forest soil or wrapped around a fixed object. This means of travel is tiring, and it is on occasions such as these that the sloth is most vulnerable to attack from predators.

sufficiently, it will not become active enough to feed and its digestive system will slow down, reducing the already slow speed at which food is absorbed.

An adult sloth has little influence on habitat selection by other sloths that overlap its range. Young three-toed sloths inherit part of their home range from their mothers, the mothers shifting their forest range slightly when the youngster is weaned. The mother has a key role to play in determining which tree species her young will use later in life, since from an early age the offspring is forcibly exposed to the female's own tree preferences. In this way, the specialization of an individual sloth on a few tree species is maintained in a population.

As a particular preference for certain sets of tree species is passed down through the generations, each line of descent—or generation of a family—of three-toed sloths has a different set of tree preferences than any other line. As a consequence of this, competition between non-related sloths for food and living space is minimized, whereas competition between sloths and other browsing leaf-eating species, such as howler monkeys, is maximized. Sloth populations reach their highest densities in forests that have high numbers of tree species; such diversity has permitted a variety of genealogical groups of sloths to evolve. ∎

LIFE CYCLE

In keeping with their relaxed attitude to life, sloths seem equally unspecific when it comes to breeding. It is difficult even to determine the sex of a sloth, since the male's scrotum is not externally visible. There does not seem to be a fixed mating season in sloths—births of two-toed sloths have been recorded in all months of the year except April, September, and November—and it is thought likely that scent plays a role in attracting a mate. It is also believed that a system of delayed implantation may operate, a system that allows the single young to be born when there is an abundant supply of food.

The mating process is a simple affair; the partners hang from a branch by their arms and turn to face each other to copulate. The gestation period varies between genera; in the case of three-toed sloths it lasts about five months. Among two-toed sloths, however, the full term may be around twice as long—which is comparable to many whales.

A CAPABLE INFANT

The single young is born up in the canopy; often the female giving birth will hang at full length, anchored only by her arms. The infant is born headfirst, and at once it climbs up onto the mother's breast using its claws to clamber through her fur. The female then bites through the umbilical cord to release her baby.

A baby sloth is a perfect miniature of its parents. Having reached the safety of the mother's chest fur, it is most reluctant to relax its grip (below).

MATING,

like all other aspects of sloth life, is an arboreal affair (right). The courtship is cursory, although copulation demands some fairly impressive gymnastics.

BRANCHING OUT

As it nears a year in age, the young sloth starts to feed itself among the branches (right). Gradually the female loses interest in her charge, even acting aggressively toward it.

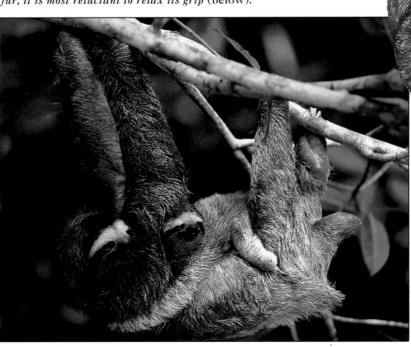

Michael Fogden/Oxford Scientific Films

Illustrations Joanne Cowne

The newly born young is precocial—fully formed at birth with ears and eyes open—and is covered in woolly fur. It is also born with a full set of brownish teeth. Despite its advanced features, however, a newborn sloth is a true miniature: It only weighs about 5 percent of the mature adult's body weight. This is significantly low compared with most other mammal species, particularly considering that the sloth bears only a single young. This low birth weight is probably explained by the sloth's arboreal existence and the relatively lean diet.

GROWING UP

The life of a young three-toed sloth

GIVING BIRTH

Gestation may last over eleven months in the two-toed sloth. The female is rewarded after this phenomenal length of time with a highly developed infant (right) that can soon take care of itself.

HOLD ON TIGHT!

Although it is weaned after only a month or so, the tiny youngster clings to its mother for several months longer. During this period of dependency (above), the female feeds it on prechewed leaves.

The birth of such a well-developed young after such a long period of pregnancy has evolved as a strategy to reduce energy needs. The long gestation avoids a rapid drain on energy, and the reduction in the duration of lactation (milk secretion) again conserves energy.

During the first four weeks of its life, the baby remains hidden within the fur of the mother who remains faithful to a small area during this period. Gradually the youngster begins to show more of an interest in its surroundings; it begins to grasp at nearby branches and sniffs at anything within reach.

A baby sloth is weaned at about one month old. At this age, it begins to take leaves that have been chewed first by the mother to reduce them into more manageable portions. At about ten weeks old, the offspring takes leaves from branches adjacent to the ones from which the mother is eating, stretching out for those it can reach from the safety of her belly. But at all times it remains close to her body, clinging to her by its legs. If for any reason the youngster is separated from its mother at this early stage in life, it gives plaintive bleating calls until they are reunited.

There are, however, rare occasions when it takes its own course in the canopy. The mother is apparently a careless climber, leaving the youngster little clearance room against the rough branches. Therefore, the infant detaches itself from its mother as she approaches obstructive branches; skirting the limb, the youngster leaps nimbly back onto the transport—nimbly, at least, for a sloth.

By nine months of age, the young sloth becomes increasingly independent and is then able to hang by itself from branches. At about this age, the mother loses interest in her offspring and will resist its approaches, even attempting to bite it if it continues to persist in its attentions. However, the young of Hoffmann's two-toed sloths have been known to associate with their mothers for up to two years after birth. The male sloth is not known to play any part in helping to rear its offspring. ■

FROM BIRTH TO DEATH

HOFFMANN'S TWO-TOED SLOTH

GESTATION: 345 DAYS

LITTER SIZE: 1

ADULT WEIGHT: 200 LB (91 KG)

WEIGHT AT BIRTH: 12–16 OZ (350–454 G)

WEANING: 3–4 WEEKS; RELIES ON MOTHER FOR 5 MONTHS

SEXUAL MATURITY: FEMALE 3.5 YEARS, MALE 4–5 YEARS

LONGEVITY: 30–40 YEARS IN WILD

BROWN-THROATED THREE-TOED SLOTH

GESTATION: 175 DAYS

LITTER SIZE: 1

ADULT WEIGHT: 100 LB (45 KG)

WEIGHT AT BIRTH: 7–9 OZ (198–255 G)

WEANING: 3–4 WEEKS; RELIES ON MOTHER FOR 6 MONTHS

SEXUAL MATURITY: 3–4 YEARS

LONGEVITY: 30–40 YEARS IN WILD

CAUTIOUS OPTIMISM

ALTHOUGH THE MANED SLOTH IS FAST RUNNING OUT OF LIVING SPACE, OTHER SPECIES OF SLOTHS SEEM TO BE WEATHERING THE SLOW RAPE OF AMAZONIA WITH MORE SUCCESS THAN MANY LARGE FOREST MAMMALS

The sloth is the subject of considerable myth among the tribespeople of Central and South American countries. The Tucuna Indians of the Brazil-Colombian border claim that the sloth let light into the world. Their story goes as follows:

"In the beginning the earth lay in darkness, cast in the shadow of a giant ceiba tree. The night monkey, immune to the darkness, climbed the tree daily and fed on parkia tree fruits. Each day as he looked up he could see a glow above him. Daily he threw parkia nut shells at the sky and gradually knocked chinks of light in the sky above—these chinks became the stars. In search of extra light, the night monkey and his brother enlisted the ants and the termites to saw down the giant ceiba tree. But the tree refused to fall even when cut all the way through—it hung suspended from the dark vaults above. So a squirrel was brought in to climb the tree and try to resolve the problem. The squirrel found a sloth using its strong grip to hold the tree upright. The squirrel threw a handful of ants into the sloth's eyes, forcing the sloth to let go its iron grip. The giant tree crashed to the ground, and there was light."

That so many stories have emerged about the sloth in Indian culture is testimony to its steady presence in forest life.

BRANDED A FREAK

Early zoologists and naturalists were rather scathing about the sloth; many regarded it as a freak of nature and of little value. Some of the earliest scientific observations of sloths go back to the early 1500s. Spanish explorer Gonzalo Fernández de Oviedo wrote, "The sloth takes the whole day for fifty paces, is about as long as it is broad, and has four thin legs with long nails, which cannot support the body. I have never seen anything uglier or more useless than the sloth." Georges-Louis Leclerc de

Buffon, a French biologist who never actually saw a sloth in its natural surroundings, described the sloth in harsh words: "The inertia of this animal is not so much due to its laziness as its wretchedness; it is the consequence of its faulty structure. Inactivity, stupidity and even habitual suffering result from its strange and ill-constructed conformation."

British naturalist Charles Waterton, who traveled in the Guianas and was one of the first naturalists to see a sloth in the field, realized just how well adapted sloths were to their virtually exclusive arboreal existence. In the 18th century, eminent biologist Carl Linnaeus considered the sloth to be closely related to the monkeys. Such status did not last and the sloths were accorded an order of their own, the *Bruta* ("the unready ones"). It was

Gregory Dimijian/Oxford Scientific Films/Photo Researchers Inc.

This sleek-looking two-toed sloth (above) *is a pet six-month-old male raised by a family near the Monteverde cloud forests in Costa Rica.*

P. J. Oxford/Planet Earth Pictures

THEN & NOW

This map shows the current distribution of Hoffmann's two-toed sloth.

DISTRIBUTION

Hoffmann's sloth is found today in tropical forests from Nicaragua in Central America through Costa Rica and Panama as far as Colombia and Ecuador in South America. There is a separate population in the western reaches of Amazonia, in northern Peru and western Brazil.

Like the closely related "true" two-toed sloth or *unau*, Hoffmann's sloth is more mobile than the three-toed sloths—but all species are still restricted to dense forest.

not until the late 1930s, when American biologists began to unravel some of the sloths' more unusual habits by observing and monitoring colonies of 50–100 sloths on Barro Colorado Island, that human beings were able to appreciate their many attributes.

Slowness of movement and an effective camouflage have made the sloths difficult to see to most eyes, let alone catch. This stillness and gray-green coloration have earned them various associations among different tribespeople. The Machiguenga Indians of the eastern Peruvian lowlands apply their word for the sloth to the shapeless twin galaxies the Magellanic Clouds. The members of the Brazilian Mundurucu tribe have a different view. When seen from a few yards away, a sloth is seen to resemble a hanging weaving. The tribespeople therefore credit the sloth with the invention of the hammock.

Unearthly and unnerving, a three-toed sloth gazes placidly from its treetop home in Amazonia.

ALONGSIDE MAN

EASYGOING PETS

Sloths are frequently taken from the wild into the household, particularly by locals in South and Central America. Two-toed sloths adapt fairly readily to life in captivity and make charming, if rather unusual, pets.

One traveler in Panama found a young two-toed sloth whose mother had died. At first reluctant to release its grip on the female, it then clung tightly to its human adoptive parent, which seemed to mollify it. The young sloth's captor then managed to keep it cozy for a while in a crate full of warmed stones. Eventually, when these cooled down, the sloth cried out for comfort and company, until it was placed in the bed of the owner's daughter. The sloth snuggled up to the girl and slept the entire night without any further distress.

This arrangement worked fine, albeit with some discomfort for the tolerant girl. Because the sloth could not regulate its own body temperature, it clung to her for warmth even on the hottest tropical nights. Fortunately, however, it soon learned not to use its claws on bare skin.

Sylvestris/Frank Lane Picture Agency

SLOTHS IN DANGER

THE MANED SLOTH IS LISTED BY THE INTERNATIONAL UNION FOR THE CONSERVATION OF NATURE (IUCN), OR THE WORLD CONSERVATION UNION, WHILE THE BROWN-THROATED AND HOFFMANN'S SLOTHS ARE LISTED BY CITES—THE CONVENTION ON INTERNATIONAL TRADE IN ENDANGERED SPECIES.

HOFFMANN'S SLOTH	CITES APPENDIX 2
BROWN-THROATED SLOTH	CITES APPENDIX 2
MANED SLOTH	ENDANGERED

CITES APPENDIX 2 INCLUDES "ALL SPECIES WHICH ALTHOUGH NOT NECESSARILY THREATENED WITH EXTINCTION AT THE PRESENT TIME MAY BECOME SO UNLESS TRADE IN SPECIMENS OF SUCH SPECIES IS SUBJECT TO STRICT REGULATION."

ENDANGERED MEANS THAT THE ANIMAL IS IN DANGER OF EXTINCTION AND ITS SURVIVAL IS UNLIKELY UNLESS STEPS ARE TAKEN TO SAVE IT.

Sloths have a peculiar but undeniable charm. They are popular not only with local Americans but also with visiting tourists.

Sloths are not overly palatable to human hunters, who complain that sloths seem to be mainly composed of hair, bone, and stringy sinew. Nonetheless there are plenty of animals willing to kill and eat sloths; tayra weasels and pumas have been seen to kill them. The sloth's best method of defense, once located, is to put as great a distance between itself and its hunter as possible. These creatures can move faster than might be expected when challenged, and they are able to dangle from thin lianas when resting or threatened, annoyingly out of the reach of predators such as arboreal cats and weasels.

A major predator is the immense harpy eagle. The world's heaviest eagle, it can grab a sloth from its protective treetop home using huge, stout talons. It can lever the hapless sloth from a branch in mid-flight and carry it off to its nest. Studies of the harpy's food debris have shown that sloths comprise the major food item in its diet. ■

INTO THE FUTURE

At present, the only species of sloth that is officially recognized as giving cause for immediate conservation concern is the maned sloth, one of the world's least-known endangered mammals.

The maned sloth lives at elevations no higher than 4,920 ft (1,500 m). Some study has been carried out on this enigmatic creature in the only area of the world in which it is found: a few sites in the states of Bahia, Espirito Santo, and Rio de Janeiro in eastern Brazil. This part of Brazil has a dense and growing human population, and the Atlantic coastal forests that once cloaked this area have been cleared for timber and charcoal production and to make way for plantations of crops such as coffee, sugarcane, and cocoa, and also for cattle pasture. Over the last twenty years this area of forest has dwindled to about 2 percent of its original Atlantic area—and even this remnant is in danger of being wiped out.

PREDICTION

A FOREST-BOUND FUTURE

Although two-toed sloths are hunted in large numbers for their flesh in many parts of South America, a far greater threat is continued forest destruction across their habitats. Sloths have taken millions of years to evolve a low energy, leaf-dependent lifestyle, and they will not be able to adapt to a life without forests.

The maned sloth still seems to occur in areas of Atlantic coastal forest that have been preserved locally, and there have been attempts to reintroduce it to areas that have been replanted with trees, such as the Tijuca National Park in Rio de Janeiro.

The maned sloth does occur naturally in nature preserves such as the Poço das Antas Biological Reserve, which was established in 1974 to help protect the extremely rare and threatened golden lion tamarin and its relatives. But even there it is found only at low densities. For example, in one survey, only fifteen individuals were counted in an area of 19 square miles (50 sq km). In addition to this, the species has an unusually fragmented range and is probably absent from several of the largest and better-protected preserves in this region, where it was until recently presumed to occur. Outside preserve areas, the maned sloth is severely threatened, not only by the continued clearance of the Atlantic coastal forests, but also by hunting. ∎

SLOTH REFUGES

The maned sloth needs additional preserves within its range, particularly in east Bahia state, one of its core areas of distribution. Within this region, there are still fairly extensive forest blocks remaining. Other endangered endemic species would benefit, such as the northern masked titi monkey and the buff-headed capuchin, both of which are also underrepresented in existing preserves. Another idea is to establish semicaptive colonies in forest areas that can be effectively protected against human activities. There is such a "free-ranging" colony at Salvador Zoo in Bahia state. As well as helping to conserve the sloths, such colonies are important for education and research.

CAPTIVITY

Although only the maned sloth is rare, the specialized lifestyles and habitat requirements of sloths put all species at risk in the long term. Unfortunately, unlike the two-toed species, three-toed sloths do not generally thrive in captivity. A problem with keeping sloths captive is that their exclusive diet of fresh leaves from rain-forest tree species is difficult to supply in sufficient quantity. In the case of the maned sloth, it has proved impossible to keep this species alive for more than a few months in captivity.

Illustration Evi Antoniou

GROUND SQUIRRELS

RELATIONS

Ground-dwelling squirrels belong to the Sciuridae family, which also includes:

RED SQUIRREL

GRAY SQUIRREL

FLYING SQUIRRELS

FOX SQUIRREL

GIANT SQUIRRELS

SUNDA SQUIRRELS

Dr. Scott Nielson/Bruce Coleman Ltd.

Ground-dwelling squirrels belong to the family Sciuridae within the suborder Sciuromorpha. The family Sciuridae, which also includes the tree squirrels, contains 267 species.

CLASS
Mammalia
(mammals)

SUBCLASS
Theria
(live-bearing mammals)

INFRACLASS
Eutheria
(placental mammals)

ORDER
Rodentia
(rodents)

SUBORDER
Sciuromorpha
(squirrel-like rodents)

FAMILIES
Sciuridae
(squirrels)

Geomyidae
(pocket gophers)

Heteromyidae
(pocket mice)

Pedetidae
(springhare)

SUBTERRANEAN SQUIRRELS

GROUND-LIVING RODENTS CAN BE FOUND IN ALMOST ANY HABITAT, IN ALMOST EVERY COUNTRY ON EARTH. SUPREMELY ADAPTABLE, THEY HAVE FORSAKEN THE TREES FOR A LIFE SPENT ON, OR UNDER, THE GROUND

Over a third of all mammal species are rodents—small, furry animals with specialized jaws and teeth. One of the largest rodent groups is the suborder Sciuromorpha, or squirrel-like rodents, which includes the terrestrial (ground-living) rodents, as well as beavers and tree-living squirrels. The terrestrial rodents belong to four families: squirrels (Sciuridae), pocket mice (Heteromyidae), pocket gophers (Geomyidae), and springhares (Pedetidae).

Ground-living rodents include ground squirrels, marmots, prairie dogs, susliks, chipmunks, pocket gophers, pocket mice, and the springhare. Although these terrestrial species have similarities that justify studying them as a group, rodent families as a whole are greatly diversified, so that the specialized front teeth and jaw action are the main common features. The Sciuromorpha also have one or two premolar teeth in each row, totaling four or five cheek teeth in each row (rats and mice have three).

Marmots live in open spaces such as pastures and steppe country (right).

Aptly named, the thirteen-lined ground squirrel is one of the more strikingly colored species (above).

Most of the ground squirrels live in burrows. Some of the ground-living squirrels, such as chipmunks, spend a lot of time away from their burrows, while others have made their burrows elaborate homes. Prairie dogs, for example, build vast subterranean towns. Most squirrels are alert and diurnal, their big eyes giving wide-angle, color vision. They are social, using a complex system of tail signals and many lively sounds.

Squirrels are absent only in Australia and New Zealand, Madagascar, southern South America, and Middle Eastern deserts. In temperate climates many of them sleep through cold weather, sometimes for half the year or longer. Only a few squirrel species, however, undergo a true hibernation.

POCKET GOPHERS AND MICE

Pocket gophers are found in North and Central America, from Saskatchewan and Manitoba in Canada to Panama in the south. They spend most of their lives in big, complex burrow systems that they dig with their chisel-like incisors and strong, broad paws. They have loose skin, like moles, so they can slip through tight tunnel spaces. Gophers live wherever the soil is soft enough to dig and where it supports rich vegetation, because roots and tubers form their main diet. Their burrows are perceived by ranchers to spoil the grassland, so great efforts are often made to exterminate these rodents. Luckily for gophers, they can reproduce rapidly.

There are lots of pocket mice, kangaroo mice, and kangaroo rats in several shapes and sizes found throughout America. Some are mouselike and live

JAW AND GNAW

The order Rodentia is divided into three suborders on the basis of the anatomy of the rodents' jaw muscles. The three divisions are the Sciuromorpha (squirrel-like rodents), the Hystricomorpha (cavylike rodents), and the Myomorpha (mouselike rodents).

The main jaw muscle is the masseter, which closes the lower jaw on the upper; it also pulls the lower jaw forward to create the gnawing action. This jaw action is unique to rodents. In the mouselike rodents the masseter has the most efficient anchorage; the Myomorpha are therefore the most successful feeders and enjoy the widest geographical distribution of all rodents.

in dense forests. Others have long hind legs and bound over deserts and arid plains. They eat seeds, insects, and other tiny prey, which they tuck away in deep, fur-lined cheek pouches.

GROUND SQUIRRELS

Most ground squirrels are a soft brown or yellowish gray color, with small, pale spots on the back and a white or yellow underside. There are exceptions, however: The thirteen-lined ground squirrel has a handsomely striped back and flanks. A ground squirrel's tail is relatively short but well furred, and the body hair can vary from soft and dense to coarse and thin, depending on the species. All ground squirrels have stumpy legs and possess large cheek pouches for

Dembinsky/Frank Lane Picture Agency

A yellow-bellied marmot basks on the rocks in the Beartooth mountains, Wyoming (above).

carrying food. They inhabit prairies, steppe, tundra, rocky country, open woodlands, or desert mountain ranges, but they are not found in dense forests. Most build burrows that can be up to 65 ft (20 m) long.

In their more southerly habitats, ground squirrels can be active all year; but in areas with a harsh climate, they hibernate in the burrow for long periods, during which they live off reserves of body fat. They may store food in their burrows but not use it until they emerge from hibernation in spring.

THE SPRINGHARE

There is just one species in the springhare family of Africa. The springhare has short forelegs, but its long hind legs power it along in kangaroolike hops of more than 10 ft (3 m). When feeding, the springhare

---

BLACK-TAILED PRAIRIE DOGS DIG TUNNELS UP TO 115 FT (35 M) LONG, LINKING THEM TO COZY NEST CHAMBERS

---

moves on all fours. But if startled, it bounds away at high speed, its long, bushy tail acting as a balance. It spends the day in its burrow, emerging at night to feed on bulbs, roots, grain, and insects. Usually several burrows are dug in the same area—some occupied by families, some by individuals.

PRAIRIE DOGS

These squirrels are short, stout animals of the open plains and plateaus in North America. All the species look alike, with a yellow-gray or buff back, paler underparts, and a tail that is usually tipped with white or black hair. Their burrows, which can be immense, are used for shelter and defense. Most species heap up mounds of excavated soil around the tunnel entrances to prevent excess surface water from entering the burrow system. These mounds are carefully tended and maintained, especially after a heavy downpour. ■

GROUND SQUIRREL
Spermophilus
(sper-mo-FILL-uss)

Ground squirrels are a collection of various rodent species from the genus Spermophilus and related genera of the rodent family Sciuridae. They occur in North America, Eastern Europe, and Asia. They are furry, have cheek pouches like chipmunks, and dig burrow homes.

SPECIES INCLUDE:
ANTELOPE GROUND SQUIRREL
LONG-CLAWED GROUND SQUIRREL

MARMOT
Marmota
(mar-MO-tah)

Marmots are burrowing sciurid rodents of the genus Marmota, found in Europe, Asia, and North America. They are heavily built, have short legs and tails, and are covered in coarse fur.

SPECIES INCLUDE:
ALPINE MARMOT
WOODCHUCK OR GROUNDHOG
YELLOW-BELLIED MARMOT

BEAVERS

FLYING SQUIRRELS

CAVYLIKE RODENTS

MOUSELIKE RODENTS

B/W illustrations Ruth Grewcock

ALL RODENTS

2086

THE PRAIRIE DOGS' FAMILY TREE

Along with the other ground-dwelling squirrels, the prairie dogs belong to the squirrel family Sciuridae. This family also includes the various tree-dwelling squirrels, such as the familiar gray and red species. Ground-dwelling rodents included in the family Sciuromorpha are the pocket mice, the pocket gophers, and the single species of springhare.

PRAIRIE DOG
Cynomys
(sy-NO-miss)

Prairie dogs are short-tailed ground squirrels that look like hamsters. They are so named because of their barking calls. They are social creatures, living together in large groups in tunnel systems. The various species are all very similar in appearance, with many habits in common. One of the best known is the way in which they stand on "sentry duty" by the entrances to their burrows. If they see a predator, they give a warning bark to the rest of their colony.

SPECIES INCLUDE:
WHITE-TAILED PRAIRIE DOG
BLACK-TAILED PRAIRIE DOG
MEXICAN PRAIRIE DOG
UTAH PRAIRIE DOG

Color illustrations Kim Thompson

GROUND-DWELLING SQUIRRELS
(SCIURIDAE)

SQUIRREL-LIKE RODENTS
(SCIUROMORPHA)

POCKET MICE

POCKET GOPHERS

SPRINGHARES

CHIPMUNK
Tamias   *Eutamias*
(TAM-ee-ass)   (yoo-TAM-ee-ass)

Chipmunks are any burrowing sciurid rodents of the genera Tamias of eastern North America and Eutamias of western North America and Asia. They often have black-striped, yellowish fur and possess cheek pouches for storing and transporting their food.

SPECIES INCLUDE:
EASTERN CHIPMUNK
SIBERIAN CHIPMUNK
MEXICAN CHIPMUNK

ANATOMY:
THE PRAIRIE DOG

Anatomy illustrations Robin Budden/Wildlife Art Agency

Terrestrial squirrel sizes range from the tiny African pygmy squirrel to the bulky Alpine marmot. The African pygmy squirrel has a head-and-body length of 2.6–4 in (6.5–10 cm), a tail length of 2–3.2 in (5–8 cm), and it weighs about 0.35 oz (10 g). The Alpine marmot has a head-and-body length of 21–29 in (53–73 cm), a tail length of 5–6.3 in (13–16 cm), and weighs about 9–18 lb (4–8 kg).

THE EYES

are large and have a highly developed retina that allows the animal to judge distances well.

THE NOSE

is prominent, with the very good sense of smell that is shared by other rodents.

THE EARS

are relatively small compared to some squirrels, presumably an adaptation to the underground lifestyle.

THE HEAD

is squirrel-like in shape, with a typically rodent jaw and dentition. The teeth are used to help with digging, as well as for feeding.

THE FORELIMBS

are rather short, but they are powerful and armed with claws for digging.

The sciurid skeleton shows that the hind legs are not more than twice the length of the forelegs, and there are four digits on each forefoot and five on each hind foot. The tail can be any length, but is usually well covered with hair and bushy. Claws are common to the ground-living squirrels and squirrel-like rodents, but the long-clawed ground squirrel has thick, powerful claws that are often more than 0.4 in (1 cm) long. No other genus except Hyosciurus has such large claws.

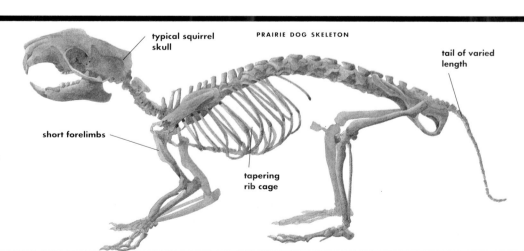

typical squirrel skull

PRAIRIE DOG SKELETON

tail of varied length

short forelimbs

tapering rib cage

X-ray illustrations Elisabeth Smith

HIND FOOT

FOREFOOT

Most rodents are plantigrade (they walk on their palms and soles). Typical to ground squirrels are the prominent claws on both forefeet and hind feet, which aid burrowing.

THE TAIL

of a squirrel-like rodent is bushy and acts as a rudder and stabilizer while the animal runs and hops from place to place. The prairie dog's tail is slightly flattened, but it is otherwise quite different from the tail of a tree squirrel. All the burrowing rodents have shorter tails than tree-living rodents.

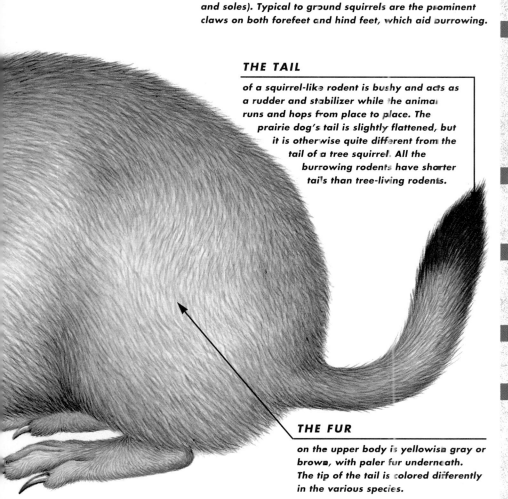

THE FUR

on the upper body is yellowish gray or brown, with paler fur underneath. The tip of the tail is colored differently in the various species.

FACT FILE:

BLACK-TAILED PRAIRIE DOG

CLASSIFICATION

GENUS: *CYNOMYS*

SPECIES: *LUDOVICIANUS*

SIZE

HEAD–BODY LENGTH: 11–13 IN (28–33 CM)

TAIL LENGTH: 1.2–4.7 IN (3–12 CM)

WEIGHT: 24.5–49 OZ (700–1,400 G)

COLORATION

GRIZZLED YELLOW-GRAY OR BUFF BACK, WITH PALER UNDERPARTS, AND A BLACK-TIPPED, SLIGHTLY FLATTENED TAIL

FEATURES

THE DISPLAY HABIT CALLED THE JUMP-YIP, COMBINING A SPECIAL LEAP INTO THE AIR AND A LOUD BARK. THIS IS USED AS A PRELUDE TO TERRITORIAL DEFENSE

13-LINED GROUND SQUIRREL

CLASSIFICATION

GENUS: *SPERMOPHILUS*

SPECIES: *TRIDECEMLINEATUS*

SIZE

HEAD–BODY LENGTH: 5–16 IN (13–41 CM)

TAIL LENGTH: 1.6–9.9 IN (4–25 CM)

WEIGHT: 3–35 OZ (85–1,000 G)

COLORATION

A SERIES OF ALTERNATING PALE AND DARK STRIPES ALONG THE BODY

FEATURES

A ROW OF PALE SPOTS IN EACH OF THE DARK BODY STRIPES

NEARLY DOUBLES IN WEIGHT BEFORE A DORMANCY THAT LASTS UP TO SEVEN MONTHS

SKULL

The sciurid skull has widely spaced eye sockets and thick, bony areas around each socket. It also has the typical rodent jaw, with just one pair of incisors on each jaw.

DENTITION

Squirrels have a small upper premolar. In some species this is lost before maturity. There are twenty or twenty-two teeth in total. The molars have roots, are low-crowned, and have enameled cusps on the lower teeth and ridges and cusps on the upper teeth.

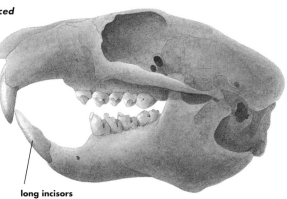

long incisors

CITIES IN THE SOIL

GROUND-LIVING SQUIRRELS ARE UNDERGROUND ARCHITECTS, AND PERHAPS THE GREATEST TOWN-PLANNERS OF ALL ARE THE PRAIRIE DOGS

A golden-mantled ground squirrel perches nimbly on a rock to drink from a pool (right).

A posse of Belding's ground squirrels stand erect on a mound, assessing the grassy plains for signs of predators (below).

Barbara Filet/Tony Stone Worldwide

T wo common habits of ground-living squirrels are their burrowing and their winter sleep. The prairie dog is a typical example. The white-tailed species hibernates throughout the late autumn and winter, whereas the black-tailed species merely becomes dormant during the winter, rather than hibernating. Neither species is known to store food in its burrow for the winter period.

Another trait common to ground-living squirrels and squirrel-like rodents is their protection of the territory around their burrows. In the breeding season, pregnant black-tailed prairie dog females that have started to produce milk for their young will nest in isolation and show hostility to the rest of the coterie, or social group. They will even try to kill and eat the young of other mothers, most of which will be breeding at the same time.

PRAIRIE DOG FEMALES DEFEND THEIR LITTERS SAVAGELY, OFTEN KILLING EVEN THE YOUNG OF OTHER, RELATED FEMALES

The white-tailed prairie dog lives in smaller and looser groups than the black-tailed species. During the breeding season, both sexes defend territories, driving off unwanted visitors, whereas in other seasons there is usually no united defense of an area. The reason for the lower density of white-tailed populations may be that they live in habitats with more protective cover than that found in black-tailed population zones, so there is less need for group surveillance of their territory.

GOPHER TUNNELS
Pocket gophers dig two types of burrows. The first is long, shallow, and winding and enables the gopher to feed on roots and tubers. The second is a

ZEFA

Throwing its head back, a prairie dog of South Dakota barks a message to its coterie (above).

accused of damaging grassland, it is more usually a case of excessive grazing by domestic cattle. The conditions caused by the cattle actually become more suitable for gopher populations, and so more rodents are attracted to the area, confusing the cause of the grassland's deterioration.

COMMUNICATION

Bonding in prairie dog groups is reinforced by kissing, nuzzling, grooming, playing together, and vocal communication. Each species makes a variety of different sounds, and one of these is the sharp sound, like a dog's bark, that gave the prairie dog its rather misleading name. This call is used during territorial confrontations.

THE MOMENT THEY HEAR THE SHRILL EMERGENCY YIP, PRAIRIE DOGS DROP EVERYTHING AND BOLT FOR COVER

Similarly, the various species of ground squirrels have a range of vocal sounds that they use in communication. These include trills, squeaks, chirps, buzzes, and a shrill whistle. This last sound is the most special, because the shrill whistle acts as an alarm. Some species use it as a warning about the approach of an airborne predator and use a chattering sound to indicate a terrestrial predator. The thirteen-lined ground squirrel growls and chatters its teeth in order to make threats. ∎

much deeper, more extensive system that provides a permanent home. It has chambers for nesting, food storage, and fecal waste. Above the ground, mounds of soil mark the extent of the tunnels, and the gophers often close off the entrances to these with more soil.

While burrowing, a gopher takes the excavated earth to the surface along sloping tunnels, holding the load between its chest and arms as it proceeds. A pocket gopher can run backward along its tunnels almost as fast as it moves forward, holding down its tail to sense the floor of the tunnel as it moves. The tunnels actually improve the condition of the ground by loosening and aerating the soil. The vegetable matter that the gopher buries also enriches the soil. In mountainous regions the tunnels carry water from melted snow deep into the ground, conserving the water and improving the condition of the soil. Whenever gophers are

HABITATS

Prairie dogs excavate their massive subterranean burrows in the open plains and plateaus in North America. Marmots also live mainly in the open habitats provided by steppes, alpine meadows, pastures, and some forest edges. Like prairie dogs, they spend most of their time underground. Their burrows are over three feet deep and up to 230–263 ft (70–80 m) long, although some hibernation burrows can be much deeper. Marmots are usually terrestrial, but occasionally they do climb into shrubs and trees, and the woodchuck, or groundhog, is known to be a good swimmer.

The woodchuck sometimes uses two sets of burrows. A winter burrow is often located on sloping ground in a wooded area, while the summer burrow is usually dug in a flatter, more open area, with a main entrance mound of freshly dug soil. The woodchuck has a different migration pattern than that of the prairie dog. In a more conventional style, it is the young woodchucks who migrate to establish their own home range when they are about three months old. They often dig temporary burrows within their home ranges and then, at a later time, head off to set up a permanent home.

In prairie dogs, however, it is the more experienced adults who migrate to new areas. The young remain in the burrows they know best. Quite often, the adults move to a territory that is already occupied, and in these cases it can take some time before they are accepted and able to establish themselves fully in the new home.

DISTRIBUTION

KEY

- HIMALAYAN MARMOT
- KAMCHATKAN MARMOT
- BOBAK MARMOT
- EUROPEAN SUSLIK
- CAPE GROUND SQUIRREL
- EAST AFRICAN GROUND SQUIRREL
- WHITE-TAILED PRAIRIE DOG
- BLACK-TAILED PRAIRIE DOG
- TERRESTRIAL SQUIRRELS

A white-tailed prairie dog on sentry duty on the plains of its homeland in Wyoming.

Franz J. Camenzind/Planet Earth Pictures

KEY FACTS

● The prairies and plains of North America once formed the greatest grasslands on Earth. They provided a source of food for an estimated 60 million bison, probably 50 million pronghorn antelope, and millions of elk and deer, as well as wolves and plains grizzly bears.

Nowadays, cash-crop farming has completely changed the character of the Great Plains and of the animals that live there.

● The Vancouver marmot is found only on tiny Vancouver Island, in British Columbia, Canada. It lives in forest clearings, high in the mountains above 3,300 feet (1,000 m).

● Menzbier's marmot is now restricted to very small areas of the Tian Shan Mountains of Uzbek and eastern Kazakhstan.

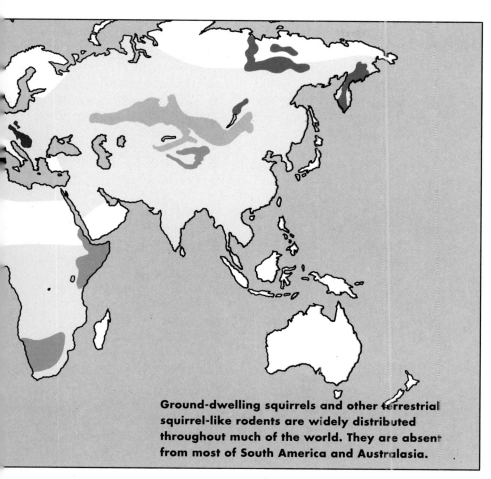

Ground-dwelling squirrels and other terrestrial squirrel-like rodents are widely distributed throughout much of the world. They are absent from most of South America and Australasia.

Anthony Bannister/NHPA

in SIGHT

ADAPTABLE RODENTS

Rodents have been successful because they are adaptable and opportunistic, exploiting almost any environmental condition to their own benefit. Rodents are an ancient order, with the oldest fossils being from the late Paleocene of North America some 50 million years ago. Many species have evolved from the original rodent design. Their ability to adapt in a number of ecological niches contributes to the fact that rodents are the most successful mammal order, representing over a third of all mammals.

The burrowing activity of ground squirrels and susliks can aerate and generally improve the condition of the land but may be a nuisance in an area where there is managed agriculture. The burrowing may even destroy or badly damage man-made irrigation channels. Other rodent activity can also be destructive: Chipmunks live in habitats where they can dig up newly planted corn seed in the spring and invade granaries in the autumn.

Rock squirrels are found only in China and comprise just two species, which some zoologists believe to be a link between the pouched chipmunks and the true squirrel species. Rock squirrels are

ROCK SQUIRRELS SHARE MANY OF THE
CHIPMUNKS' BEHAVIORAL HABITS,
ALTHOUGH THEY DO NOT HIBERNATE

extremely agile. They live on rocky, shrubby mountain cliffs, where they nest in crevices, and avoid dense forest habitats. Although they can climb trees, they prefer to move around in rocky terrain. They occasionally enter areas of human settlement in order to find food.

The Barbary ground squirrel inhabits Morocco and Algeria and was recently introduced on Fuerteventura, one of the Canary Islands. It is usually found in rocky areas, where it rests in its burrow, out of the hot midday sun. It emigrates to new regions when its population rises to a level that cannot be supported by the local habitat.

A Cape ground squirrel uses its tail as a parasol to deflect the searing heat of the midday sun in Africa's Namibian desert.

Similar squirrels are found elsewhere in Africa but represent a different genus, *Xerus*. There are four species of African ground squirrels, and between them they inhabit Sudan, Tanzania, Morocco, Mauritania, Senegal, Kenya, Namibia, Botswana, Zimbabwe, South Africa, and Angola. These squirrels live in open woodland, grassland, or rocky country and dig burrow homes.

The long-clawed ground squirrel is found only in Soviet central Asia, near the Caspian Sea, and in northern Afghanistan and Iran. This species lives in small family groups in sandy deserts, where it digs its burrows among brushy vegetation. It will travel over half a mile (1 km) if there is little food to be found near its home, but it saves most of this activity for cooler periods of the day.

Western pocket gophers of the genus *Thomomys* are found in Canada and western and central North America. Eastern pocket gophers, genus *Geomys*, are found in central and eastern North America. *Thomomys* species inhabit areas with many soil types, from sea level to altitudes of about 13,000 ft (4,000 m). These areas include deserts, prairies, meadows, and open forests. *Geomys* species prefer loose and sandy soil in open or sparsely wooded regions, but gopher tunnels do cause soil

erosion on hillsides in these favored areas. Where the eastern pocket gopher lives in farmland, it often damages crops, either by feeding on them directly or by covering the plants with its mounds.

Taltuzas (genus *Orthogeomys*) and the single species of tuza, *Zygogeomys trichopus*, are found only in Mexico and Central America. Taltuzas inhabit a variety of terrains, from arid tropical lowlands to mountain forests at altitudes of around 10,000 feet (3,000 m). The tuza has a more restricted habitat. It lives in areas of deep, soft, and yielding soil in conifer forests that are located at altitudes above 7,000 feet (2,200 m). ■

FOCUS ON

THE GREAT PLAINS

To the west of the Appalachian mountains, there is an extensive eastern forest dominated by broad-leaved, deciduous trees. Beyond this to the west, the forest originally merged into prairies that were dominated by plants and grasses such as big bluestem and Indian grass. These have been replaced to a great extent by corn and soybean fields planted in recent times by humans. These tall-grass prairies change to mixed-grass prairies as one moves farther west because of the effects of lower rainfall.

Eventually these change to short-grass plains, which stretch to the Rocky Mountains. The plains are covered by buffalo grass and little grama grass. The short-grass plains were the home of the vast bison herds that were devastated by settler hunting and by the use of the land for grazing.

railroads that cut through the original vegetation.

Escape from predators on these open grasslands is difficult for small mammals. Animals such as the prairie dog use burrows to avoid the coyotes, eagles, buzzards, and foxes that are their natural predators. The burrowing owl, too, nests in the prairie dogs' burrows because of the lack of suitable sites above ground.

TEMPERATURE AND RAINFALL

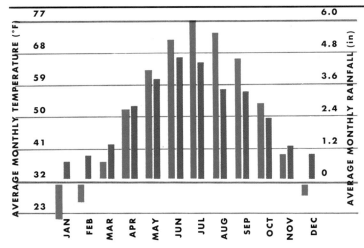

TEMPERATURE
RAINFALL

The eastern third of the Great Plains has about 30 in (76 cm) of rain each year. Farther west the rainfall drops, and the vegetation is lower in growth. Temperatures on the Plains can vary by more than 144°F (80°C) throughout the year.

NEIGHBORS

The Great Plains are rich feeding grounds for many herbivores, from the tiny prairie dog to the massive bison. Like all grazers, these animals attract predators, too.

BISON

Vast herds of bison once roamed the prairies but were exploited to near extinction.

INDIGO SNAKE

This nonpoisonous snake of North America is a lustrous blue-black in color.

Illustrations Joanne Cowne

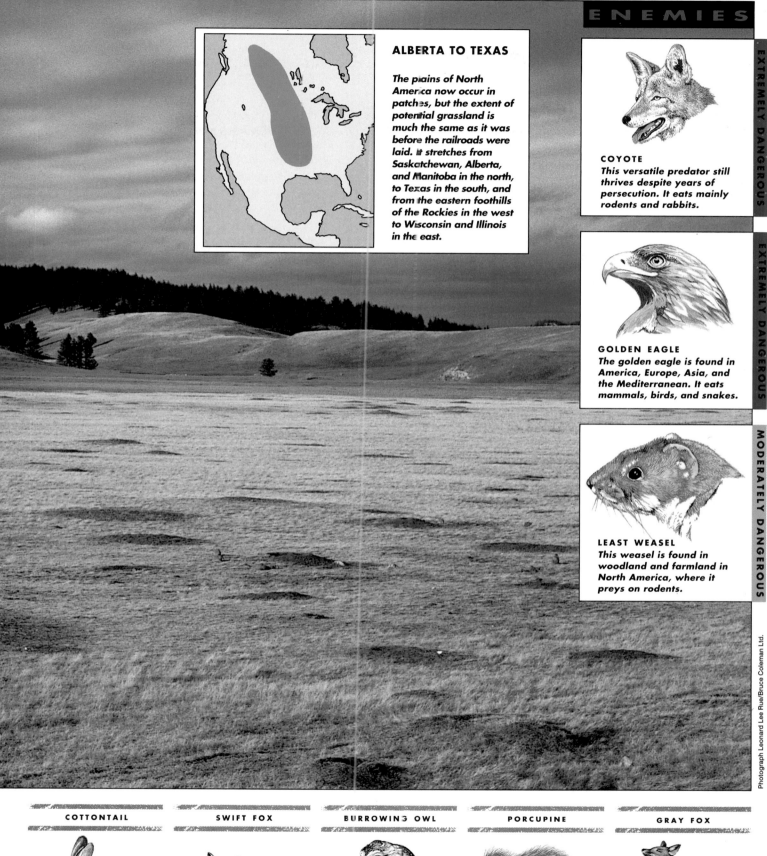

ALBERTA TO TEXAS

The plains of North America now occur in patches, but the extent of potential grassland is much the same as it was before the railroads were laid. It stretches from Saskatchewan, Alberta, and Manitoba in the north, to Texas in the south, and from the eastern foothills of the Rockies in the west to Wisconsin and Illinois in the east.

ENEMIES

Photograph Leonard Lee Rue/Bruce Coleman Ltd.

EXTREMELY DANGEROUS

COYOTE
This versatile predator still thrives despite years of persecution. It eats mainly rodents and rabbits.

EXTREMELY DANGEROUS

GOLDEN EAGLE
The golden eagle is found in America, Europe, Asia, and the Mediterranean. It eats mammals, birds, and snakes.

MODERATELY DANGEROUS

LEAST WEASEL
This weasel is found in woodland and farmland in North America, where it preys on rodents.

COTTONTAIL

There are several American rabbit species. The desert cottontail is a typical example of a plains rabbit.

SWIFT FOX

This rare, cat-sized fox lives on the western plains. It can run fast and sometimes preys on prairie dogs.

BURROWING OWL

American burrowing owls often nest in old prairie dog burrows on the Great Plains.

PORCUPINE

The North American porcupine keeps mainly to the forests, but it ventures to grassy areas in summer.

GRAY FOX

This short-legged fox is a skillful tree-climber. It is a wily and elusive farmland predator.

SOCIAL STRUCTURE

Erwin & Peggy Bauer/Bruce Coleman Ltd.

lives alone in its own den, although it is still part of the larger colony. Prairie dogs' social behavior, however, is surprisingly refined, with the animals living together in a highly organized society. Each of their basic social units, or coteries, associates with neighboring coteries to build an extended "town" that might cover a territory of over 250 acres (100 ha). Coteries contain an average of eight to nine animals, and they all collectively defend their territory.

All the coterie burrows are linked to give space for refuge, for rearing the young, for day-to-day living and socializing, and for hibernating. The entrances to the burrows are normally surrounded

Black-tailed prairie dogs (left) *enjoy the protection of close-knit family units called coteries.*

Many of the terrestrial squirrels are highly social, living in colonies of assorted sizes. Furthermore, many species spend all their adult lives within fairly limited home ranges. The home range is very important: Becoming totally familiar with it can save an animal's life, since it then knows where to take refuge from predators and where to find its food. Some predators can follow the rodent into its burrow, and then it is vital to know where escape exits lie. Because the home range is so important, the rodent must establish and "map" one as early in life as it can. It achieves this by exploring its surroundings from an early age.

ALPINE MARMOTS USE A HIGH-ALTITUDE BURROW SYSTEM IN SUMMER, MOVING DOWN THE MOUNTAIN SLOPES IN WINTER

One example of the social structure is provided by the Alpine marmot, which lives in a colony of two to fifty or more animals in a large burrow system that they have dug. Once the marmots have built their burrow network, they do not travel far from it. They live in, and protect, an area of about 0.6 acres (0.25 ha) in their mountain environment. They mark out the territory with scent secreted from glands in their cheeks and chase away intruders, gnashing their teeth and uttering loud calls as aggressive signals.

The prairie dog is possibly the most social of terrestrial squirrels, occupying extensive burrow systems, but susliks and ground squirrels also live in social colonies. The European suslik actually

UNDERGROUND WORLD

The underground world of the prairie dog consists of sets of cleverly constructed tunnels and special areas for carrying out the daily routines of life. The special areas are usually built as chambers that are set off to the sides of the main tunnels. This allows the prairie dog an unimpeded route when it needs to escape rapidly from predators.

Illustrations Phillip Hood/Wildlife Art Agency

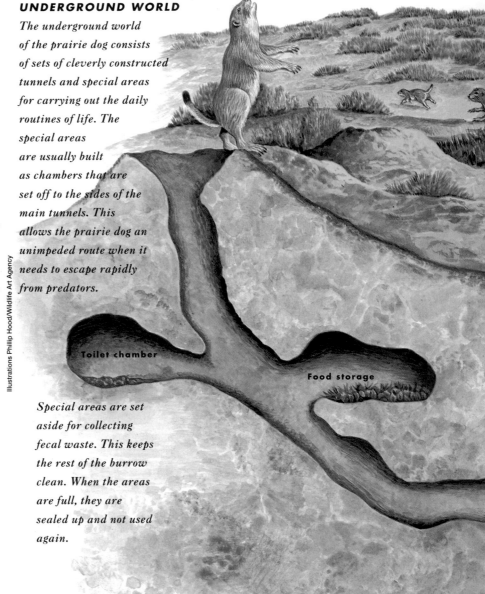

Toilet chamber

Food storage

Special areas are set aside for collecting fecal waste. This keeps the rest of the burrow clean. When the areas are full, they are sealed up and not used again.

in SIGHT

GREETINGS, FRIEND!

The greeting "kiss" helps reduce hostility between members of a prairie dog family and enables strangers to be detected. When two animals meet they squat low and crawl forward. They then bare their teeth and kiss—unless they are strangers, in which case they retreat or tussle. If the animals know each other, one may nibble and groom the other. This helps prairie dogs bond, and all coterie members groom one another. The animals may then feed together. As well as kisses, quick pecks are used to confirm identity and to keep the peace.

Rod Planck/NHPA

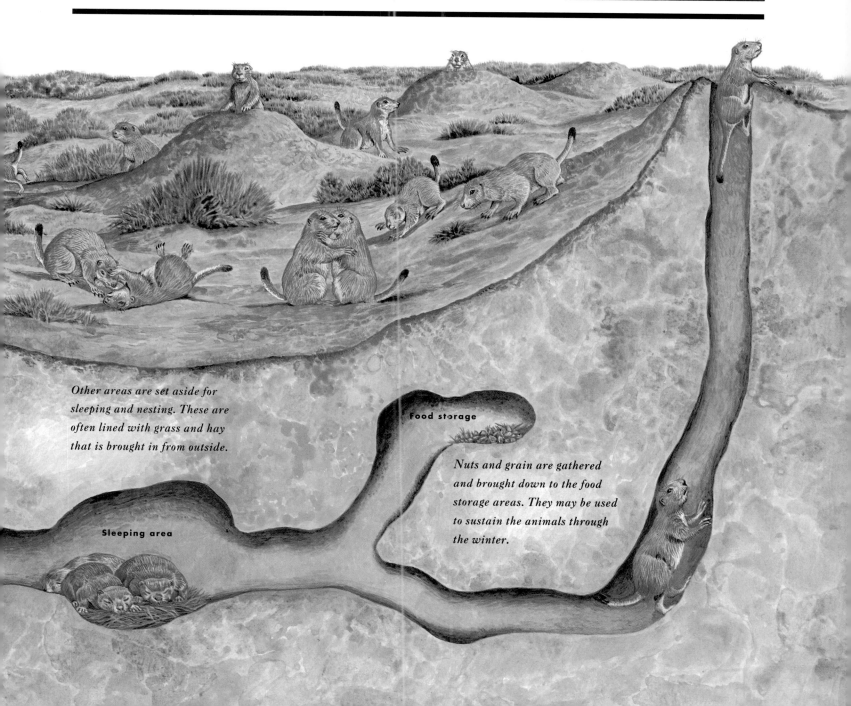

Other areas are set aside for sleeping and nesting. These are often lined with grass and hay that is brought in from outside.

Food storage

Nuts and grain are gathered and brought down to the food storage areas. They may be used to sustain the animals through the winter.

Sleeping area

GOPHERS GALORE

Pocket gophers live in North America, from western Canada south to the Panama and Colombian border, and from coast to coast where habitats suitable for digging occur—for they are excellent burrowers.

The pocket gopher has strong forearms, and each forepaw has five claws. While it is digging it can easily get dirt in its eyes, so these are equipped with tear glands that supply plenty of viscous tears to keep the cornea clean. Like other rodents, it can close its lips behind its teeth when gnawing to keep dirt from getting into its mouth.

These little animals do not travel far but spend most of their time underground (although they do not hibernate). Their burrows provide vital escape routes from their many enemies, which include badgers, coyotes, and foxes, as well as owls, which prey on them at night.

Tom McHugh/Oxford Scientific Films

by mounds of earth to prevent water from entering, and possibly flooding, the burrow system.

When prairie dogs meet they use a set of actions to greet and to confirm each other's identity. They often start off by touching noses, but some of their social behavior is more complex. The territory is defended by a dominant male—which may chase and call out to prairie dogs from another coterie—and sometimes by the male's mate, which also calls aggressively to repel intruders. In coteries where there is no breeding activity, there may be several males and females, with one male dominating the other males, but with no female hierarchy. When breeding is taking place, there is one male adult for

---

PRAIRIE DOGS ARE AMONG THE MOST SOCIAL OF TERRESTRIAL SQUIRRELS, PARTICULARLY WHEN BREEDING

---

every four adult females, plus several juveniles a year or two old. There is also a seasonal change in the relationship between coteries. This swings from an open and relaxed boundary system in the summer, when contact between coterie populations is friendly, to a rigid and exclusive territorial arrangement in the autumn and winter, when the dominant male is actively protecting boundaries. The territorial aggression relaxes again the following spring so that coterie socializing and interbreeding can occur again.

SPRINGHARE

The springhare, *Pedetes capensis*, lives in dry savanna and semidesert. It is the single species within its family, found only in southern and eastern Africa, south of the Sahara. It grazes at night and spends all day underground in its burrow. A substantial animal, the springhare weighs 6.5–9 lb (3–4 kg) and has an upright posture when still. Its long hind legs make it an excellent jumper. It has a long furry coat that is rusty brown with some long black hairs, and it has whiter underparts. The latter half of its tail is black.

The springhare's forefeet have five toes with long, sharp claws, and its hind feet have four toes with nail-like claws. It uses its foreclaws to dig its burrow, or warren, which can stretch for up to 295–330 ft (90–100 m). The warren often has four or five entrances and may be home to a colony of springhares, although it seems that each animal has its own sleeping area.

The springhare crouches down to feed, eating roots, bulbs, grain, and other plant material, and takes crops from cultivated areas to supplement its diet. Many reports indicate that the springhare will travel considerable distances in search of food, possibly up to twelve and a half miles (20 km) in a night. It travels by leaping along, bounding over distances of roughly 5 ft (1.5 m) at each pace.

Illustration Evi Antoniou

If the coterie becomes overcrowded at any time, the adults move out to expand the town boundary. This leaves more room for the young. Ultimately, however, juvenile males usually leave their coterie and try to enter and control another one.

The social behavior of marmots varies greatly. The woodchuck is very competitive and is the most solitary of the marmot genus, but it may share a burrow with a female and join other woodchucks to feed. However, the aggressive adults force their offspring away from the home by the time they are only six or seven weeks old.

The yellow-bellied marmot is much more social. Its units comprise one adult male and two or three closely related females. Several units may join to form a larger group, but the males each defend its own unit's territory. The young males are forced from the home after two summers, when they are just over one year old. About half of the young females remain with their home unit.

The African rock squirrels behave much like the prairie dogs. They guard the area around their burrows, they interact with their neighbors, they sun themselves, they noisily chase away intruders,

POCKET MICE

Robert Erwin/NHPA

Pocket mice live from Canada south to South America. Four genera look like mice, and two genera have long hind legs for jumping, using the tail for balance. All pocket mice have long, hairy tails, and, like pocket gophers, they have cheek pouches for carrying food. These rodents favor deserts or humid tropical forests and, although physically unsuited to life underground, dig their own burrows. They stay at home during the day, sometimes closing themselves inside by plugging the entrance with moist earth. In winter they stay below ground and can become dormant during extreme cold. They take most of their water from their food, and some species are adapted to conserve water within the body.

they feed near their burrow, and they rush back to their burrow if in danger. Various birds and carnivores, including the small viverrid mongoose, prey on these squirrels if they are able, although one species of rock squirrel sometimes shares its burrows with another viverrid species, the meerkat.

Not all rock squirrels are social, however. One species in Kenya lives in isolated burrow systems; it does not guard a territory or form social groups, other than mother-young associations. All the rock squirrels can be tamed, and in South Africa they are often kept as pets. Farmers, however, treat them as pests because they attack corn, sweet potato, bean,

TAMED ROCK SQUIRRELS IN SOUTH AFRICAN HOMES ARE SAID TO BEHAVE MUCH LIKE DOMESTIC CATS

and other crops. More seriously, they can carry diseases such as bubonic plague and rabies.

Although pocket gophers also build burrows, they usually live alone and are intolerant of other pocket gophers. Outside the breeding season, two adults usually fight if they are placed together. Gophers do not hibernate but may become almost dormant in colder regions during winter. However, they do move about in winter and will tunnel through the snow if it has fallen over their burrow area. Sometimes they carry earth from their lower burrows into these snow tunnels. ∎

FOOD AND FEEDING

All rodents have characteristic teeth, including a single pair of extremely sharp incisors that are used for gnawing through the toughest of husks, pods, and nuts to get to the nutritious seed contents. Rodents have no canine teeth but do have many heavily enameled molar teeth for grinding down their food.

Terrestrial squirrels feed most of the time on low-growing plants. Like rabbits, they can have a marked effect on the amount and style of the vegetation around the areas where they live. Prairie dogs, for example, feed in the immediate vicinity of their burrows and always keep the tunnel entrances clear of obstructions in order to have the best view of the surrounding area, and hence of any predators. To do this, they bite down all the

---

MARMOTS EAT GRASSES AND OTHER GREEN VEGETATION, GRAINS, BEANS, PEAS, FRUITS, AND INSECTS

---

nearby tall grass or plants and feed on grass and herbs. However, they are careful to practice crop rotation—reaping food from different areas in turn to allow each patch to regenerate. They get all the water they need from this vegetation, as do most other squirrels. These grazing habits result in mainly fast-growing plants around their burrows.

LAYING UP WINTER STORES
Ground squirrels that hibernate prepare for the big sleep by building up food supplies below ground. The Siberian chipmunk can carry about a third of an ounce (10 g) of food in its cheek pouches and travel half a mile (1 km) or more before storing it. The food may be grain, seeds, buds, acorns, or mushrooms. These foodstuffs are stored in different compartments of its underground home, next to its sleeping chamber. Each chipmunk can store up to 11–13 lb (5–6 kg) of food for the winter.

Ground squirrels and susliks also fatten up before their hibernation, which lasts from five to seven months. In addition, they store winter food

supplies that are usually eaten only after the animals come out of hibernation. The hoary marmot lives in the mountainous areas of Alaska and northern Canada. During the summer it, too, builds up fat reserves, comprising up to one-fifth of its body weight, that it uses to survive the winter. This is a common feature of many marmot species.

Like many other squirrels, the long-clawed ground squirrel eats bulbs, seeds, fruit, plants, and insects. It does not, however, live in cultivated regions, so it is not normally considered to be a pest

Guy Troughton/Wildlife Art Agency

GRASSES AND ROOTS,
as well as nuts and grains, are eaten by prairie dogs. Eating is carried out feverishly just before the onset of winter.

FOOD

GRASSHOPPER	COUCH GRASS	PINE NUTS	PURPLE CONEFLOWER	DANDELION
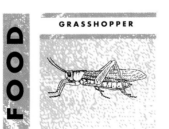	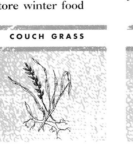			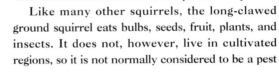

Food illustrations Ruth Grewcock

TO VARY ITS

diet, the African ground squirrel takes advantage of the local plant life by eating cactus flowers.

to farmers. It will attack and eat plants that encroach on its habitat and that may have been planted to bind the loose, sandy terrain.

The pocket gopher has two long, fur-lined pouches extending from its face back to its shoulders. These are used to carry food; they can be turned inside out for cleaning and are pulled back into place by a special muscle. It has a total of twenty teeth, and its cheek teeth grow throughout

its life to compensate for the wear caused by grinding. It rarely drinks water, getting enough moisture from the vegetation it eats.

Western pocket gophers eat roots and bulbs, leaves, grains, and other vegetation. Some of the eastern pocket gopher species eat rhizomes and roots, as well as succulent surface vegetation if it is easily reached from the burrow. They also bite down the stems of plants and carry them in their pouches to storage areas in the burrows. Some of this food may be put aside for winter use.

Prairie dogs and other terrestrial squirrels do not endear themselves to farmers by eating grasses or crops; these foodstuffs are important to livestock or as farming produce. As a result, these rodents have suffered a long history of persecution. ◼

PINECONES

provide part of the diet of the eastern American chipmunk.

in SIGHT

NUTCRACKER SWEET

Nuts and seeds are a highly nutritious dietary element for many squirrels. Like so many rodents, these sharp-toothed animals have developed an effective levering technique for opening nuts, and they can consume masses of nuts each day.

The squirrel grips the nut with both hands and its upper incisors and gnaws a hole in the shell using its lower incisors and powerful jaw muscles. The lower teeth are then used as a lever to split the shell neatly in half. Young squirrels soon learn to select only good nuts and throw away the bad.

LIFE CYCLE

For ground-living squirrels, every aspect of breeding is connected with the sense of smell. Odors—probably gland-based scents called pheromones—influence all elements of reproduction, from first attraction to the departure of young from the family home.

Most squirrels can breed at one year old. The gestation period in squirrels is quite short: only three to six weeks. All infant squirrels are born without teeth and with their eyes closed, but by the time they are six weeks old, they are furred and are capable enough to leave the burrow. Usually the

PRAIRIE DOG COTERIES INTERMINGLE DURING BREEDING SEASON, DIMINISHING THE CHANCE OF MATING WITH CLOSE RELATIVES

female alone is responsible for parental care of the young, while the father often leaves the home altogether after mating. In some ground-living rodents, such as prairie dogs and marmots, however, both sexes nurture their offspring, especially while the pups are playing or exploring outside the burrow. The young seem to respond to this parental care by staying in the burrow through the next hibernation and the next summer.

Marmots can breed from one year old, although they mature fully at two. They usually mate within

A golden-mantled ground squirrel (below) sleeps through the winter in a nest of dried grasses.

THE MOTHER
raises the young, unaided by other members of the coterie. However, the young pups do suckle from any lactating females in the group and they are gently groomed by any male in the coterie. The pups' eyes open after about thirty-three days, and this is when they first start to venture out of the burrow.

THE FEMALE GIVES BIRTH
to a litter of usually four pups in March, April, or May. The young are born with their eyes closed. The mother suckles the young pups until they are weaned, which is normally within about seven weeks.

Jeff Foott/Bruce Coleman Ltd.

THE COTERIE

is the prairie dog's basic family unit. In a breeding coterie, there is usually one adult male for every four adult females, with a few young or juveniles. A female mates with a male from the coterie or from a nearby group, and if she becomes pregnant she will produce one litter in the year.

THE NEST IS BUILT

in one of the burrows using material carried in from the outside. Pregnant and lactating females nest alone and are hostile to any approaches from the other members of the unit. Gestation takes about five weeks.

All illustrations Simon Turvey/Wildlife Art Agency

a few days of leaving their winter home. Gestation takes five weeks, and the pregnant female seals off her nesting area with grass and hay a few days before the birth to secure a little privacy.

Prairie dog pups can take up to about 15 months to grow to adult size, breeding only when they reach about two years old. Unusual for rodents, mature females bear only one litter a year.

The breeding habits of the various species of African rock squirrel differ, but they are basically typical of squirrels. Some breed all year, while others have a defined breeding season. Their litters may vary from two to six pups, and the young are sexually mature at about one year old. The long-clawed ground squirrel of central Asia mates during February and March and gives birth to between three and six young in April or May.

For gophers, the mating season is about the only time when the animals socialize. Female western pocket gophers have one litter each year; they mate during April or early May in Canada, and in July and August in colder mountain areas. After a gestation period of 18–19 days, usually three or four young are born. The young stay in the burrow for about two months before moving on to new areas. They reach adult weight at about five months and become sexually mature within a year.

Female eastern pocket gophers may have more than one litter each year, especially in the warmer states. In these cases the litter size is usually smaller. The newborn weigh about 0.2 oz (5 g). Their eyes open at 22–23 days; they are weaned at 28–35 days and leave their mother at about seven weeks (49 days). ∎

FROM BIRTH TO DEATH

BLACK-TAILED PRAIRIE DOG
GESTATION: 34–37 DAYS
LITTER SIZE: USUALLY 4
EYES OPEN: 5 WEEKS
WEANED: AFTER 7 WEEKS

INDEPENDENCE: 15 MONTHS
SEXUAL MATURITY: 18–24 MONTHS
LIFE SPAN IN WILD: NOT WELL KNOWN IN WILD, BUT UP TO 8.5 YEARS IN CAPTIVITY

BELDING'S GROUND SQUIRREL
GESTATION: 23–31 DAYS
LITTER SIZE: 1–15, USUALLY 5
EYES OPEN: NOT KNOWN
WEANED: 4–6 WEEKS

INDEPENDENCE: 5–7 WEEKS
SEXUAL MATURITY: 11–15 MONTHS
LIFE SPAN IN WILD: TYPICALLY 2–3 YEARS FOR MALES, 3–4 YEARS FOR FEMALES; SOME LIVE 6–10 YEARS

PESTS OF THE PLAINS

CUTE THEY MAY BE, BUT THESE CHARACTERS WIN NO MERCY FROM FARMERS. THIS CENTURY HAS WITNESSED A GRIM HARVEST OF SQUIRRELS. SOME HAVE FOUGHT BACK, OTHERS HAVE BEEN LESS LUCKY

P rairie dog populations increased rapidly in the late 19th century because their natural predators were reduced or eliminated by people migrating west across the United States. Other animals, such as the bison, competed for the prairie dog's food, but because these animals were hunted by man, the result was more food for the prairie dog.

Some people believe that it was the introduction of domestic cattle into some areas that improved the habitat by keeping the vegetation low and quick-growing. Whatever the reasons, prairie dogs multiplied at such a rate that by the early 1900s they were so numerous that they started to cause economic problems by feeding on

Jeff Foott/Survival Anglia

> OVER A 75-YEAR PERIOD SINCE THE START OF THE CENTURY, PRAIRIE DOG NUMBERS IN SOME PARTS OF THE UNITED STATES HAD BEEN REDUCED BY A FACTOR OF 300–400

Thawed after the winter, these tunnels reveal how gophers bring soil deep into snow tunnels (above).

farm crops and pasture. This led to a widespread campaign in North America to destroy as many of them as possible. Public and private projects were set up to poison the animals, which led to a substantial reduction in prairie dog numbers.

Even so, today the black-tailed prairie dog is not rare; but if the poisoning programs were restarted, the species would be seriously threatened. The poisoning has taken its toll on various other prairie dog species, such as the Utah prairie dog, which has been so severely reduced that it is now considered vulnerable. The Mexican prairie dog is considered threatened as a result of both poisoning and extensive farming activities.

Ground squirrel populations around the world have suffered the same fate. As in the case of the prairie dog, the thirteen-lined ground squirrel

increased in its range and numbers at first, as its habitat was cleared by man's deforestation and agriculture. In Canada, ground squirrels increased so rapidly that they became one of the most serious pests through their excessive feeding on crops. In the end, poisoning was also used to control ground squirrels. Some hunting also helps control the population, and the pelts of some ground squirrels are used for clothing.

The rock squirrel has been classified as a vulnerable species in southern China because of man's destruction of its habitat. In a similar way, the numbers of many eastern pocket gopher species have plummeted during this century because of changes in the way man uses and treats the animals' habitat.

Karl Switak/NHPA

As well as providing meat and fur for Mexicans, ground squirrels are also kept as pets (right).

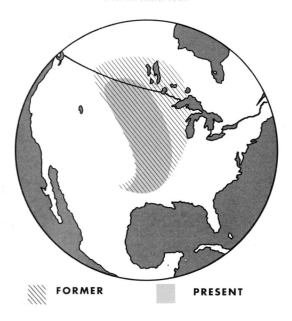

The map shows both the former and present distribution of the black-tailed prairie dog in North America.

FORMER   PRESENT

The area of North America inhabited by the black-tailed prairie dog has been reduced dramatically during this century. Good examples are provided by the states of South Dakota and Kansas. In South Dakota the inhabited area has shrunk by a factor of over 30 to just 93 sq miles (240 sq km), and in Kansas by a factor of 70 to an even smaller 58 sq miles (150 sq km).

Although severely limited today in its distribution, and having suffered extermination programs, this species is not considered to be under threat.

Halle Flygare Photos Ltd./Bruce Coleman Ltd.

A Columbian ground squirrel burrow in Banff National Park, Canada (above).

Spichtinger/ZEFA

Rodents and people have a long association that ranges from adulation to hatred.
At one extreme, some species are looked
on with affection, especially squirrels
with their "cute" appearance. Marmots
were taught to perform at medieval fairs,
prairie dogs and woodchucks appear in
the legends of the American Indians, and
pocket gophers have been tamed and
kept in captivity. At the other extreme,
however, squirrels and marmots are
hunted as game animals and for their
pelts, and prairie dogs are poisoned in
large numbers to reduce populations.
This type of treatment stems from the
damage that rodents can cause to crops,
trees, and human food stores.

An inquisitive Alpine marmot investigates a hiker's backpack in Austria.

Studies in the late 1970s and early 1980s revealed
that some species and subspecies in Georgia, on the
east coast of Florida, and on the coast of Mexico
were near, or had already suffered, extinction.

Chipmunks seem to have coped with man's
incursion into their natural habitats. In the eastern
United States and southeast Canada, the eastern
chipmunk is still quite common—it apparently causes
little crop damage. It is often destroyed by poisoning
if numbers become excessive, and sometimes it is
hunted for its fur. Studies in the mid-1980s suggested
that localized populations could become extinct
through excessive habitat alteration. This means that
in agricultural areas it is vital to preserve connected

stretches of woodland. Things may be a little worse
for the Siberian and western American chipmunks,
which cause more damage to crops and trees in their
search for food and so are considered pests.

Some marmot species first reacted to man-made
habitat changes in similar ways to prairie dogs and
ground squirrels. The woodchuck first multiplied in
numbers and then was hunted and poisoned when
it came to be seen as a nuisance. Later on, from the

SKI RESORT DEVELOPMENT IN
VANCOUVER HAS AFFECTED LOCAL
MARMOTS, WHICH ARE NOW PROTECTED

late 1970s to the mid-1980s, there were several
detailed studies about the environmental impact on
other marmot species.

Taltuzas and the tuza are also threatened. All
taltuza species are treated as pests in certain habitats because they damage crops. Poisoning, hunting,
and habitat change have all taken their toll. In
Mexico they are often killed by professional catch-
ers, *tuceros*, who are hired by local farmers. A
bounty is paid for each animal caught, an arrangement that presumably is profitable to the farmers,
who otherwise find that their papaya, banana,
corn, or sugarcane crops are spoiled. Some locals
eat taltuza meat as a delicacy, but this contributes
only in a small way to the depletion of these gopher
species. The tuza's wooded habitat is being cleared
by humans; this has encouraged other gopher
species to encroach upon its territory, and the tuza
seems unable to compete. The tuza may be close to
extinction because of all these influences. ■

SQUIRRELS IN DANGER

THE INTERNATIONAL UNION FOR THE CONSERVATION OF NATURE'S
RED DATA BOOK LISTS THE FOLLOWING TERRESTRIAL SQUIRREL SPECIES:

MEXICAN PRAIRIE DOG	ENDANGERED
UTAH PRAIRIE DOG	VULNERABLE
MENZBIER'S MARMOT	VULNERABLE
VANCOUVER ISLAND MARMOT	ENDANGERED
SOUTHERN POCKET GOPHER	RARE
MICHOACAN POCKET GOPHER	INDETERMINATE

THE *RED DATA BOOK* ALSO INCLUDES TWO CHIPMUNK, EIGHT
RAT KANGAROO, AND THREE POCKET MOUSE SPECIES.

Nicholas Parfitt/Tony Stone Worldwide

INTO THE FUTURE

On the whole, the future does not seem too gloomy for the ground-living squirrels and squirrel-like rodents. However, special action is needed to ensure the survival of a few threatened species. Most at risk is the Vancouver Island marmot, which is found only in the mountains and in forest clearings above the tree line. Ski-resort development and logging have severely reduced its numbers to only a few hundred. British Columbia now protects this species by law, and there may be reserves set aside for it in the future.

Other species at special risk include the big-eared kangaroo rat, the Utah prairie dog, the Mexican prairie dog, the Menzbier's marmot, the Bobak marmot, and the European suslik.

The European suslik used to be abundant in the steppe of east and southeast Europe, and it spread as far east as the Crimea. Then human agricultural activity started to have a serious impact on its steppe

PREDICTION

HOPE ON THE HORIZON

The steppe marmot has a great potential range for habitation; it can adapt to farmland and exploit suitable niches. The recovery in its numbers indicates that its chances are improving.

habitat and its numbers are now reduced substantially, especially in Hungary. However, there are some higher-altitude areas in the former Yugoslavia and Czechoslovakia where agriculture has not encroached on its territory, and locally it remains quite common.

Also in eastern Europe, the Bobak marmot has experienced similar problems because of agricultural development, but in addition it has been hunted for its fur. As a result, the future looks uncertain for this steppe marmot.

The marmot used to occur across an area that extended east from the steppes of eastern Europe through Kazakhstan, Mongolia, and western China. However, it is now extinct in several parts of eastern Europe, including Hungary, Romania, and Poland. Its numbers continue to decline in some areas where its steppe habitat is still threatened, but it is regaining territories by colonizing abandoned farming areas and by some specific reintroduction programs. ■

PROTECTION PLANS

Most of the risk to ground-living squirrels and squirrel-like rodents is due to either habitat damage caused by humans or extermination programs that are aimed at reducing levels of crop damage caused by the rodents. Luckily for this group of species, they are relatively minor pests compared to some rats and mice—particularly the Norway, common, and roof rats and the house mouse—so they are less persecuted by humans. Even so, some species are still considered to be serious pests, and these include the prairie dogs, marmots, and ground squirrels of the California and Mongolian grasslands.

Happily for the ground-living, squirrel-like populations, the scale of the extermination projects has been reduced since the 1970s. Today it may be the changes to local habitats that represent the biggest threat. Unfortunately the impact of these habitat changes comes at a time when several species are already seriously weakened in numbers by the earlier exterminations. Preservation and recovery projects will be important in the future for these especially vulnerable species. In the last twenty years or so there have already been several captive-breeding and reintroduction programs set up for some endangered species of terrestrial squirrels. Hopefully, these initiatives will prevent any future possibility of the extinction of these species.

Illustration Evi Antoniou

TREE SQUIRRELS

Tree squirrels belong to the order Rodentia and the squirrel family, Sciuridae. Other squirrels include:

ALPINE MARMOT

HOARY MARMOT

GROUND SQUIRRELS

LITTLE SOUSLIK

EUROPEAN SOUSLIK

SIBERIAN CHIPMUNKS

PRAIRIE DOGS

Manfred Danegger/NHPA

The squirrel family is the largest of several families within the diverse group of squirrel-like rodents. The family comprises ground squirrels, tree squirrels, and flying squirrels. The 26 genera of tree squirrels contain 132 species, while the 14 genera of flying squirrels contain 37 species.

ORDER
Rodentia
(rodents)

SUBORDER
Sciuromorpha
(squirrel-like rodents)

FAMILY
Sciuridae
(squirrels)

TREE SQUIRRELS GENERA

Tamiasciurus, Callosciurus, Sciurus, Ratufa, etc

FLYING SQUIRRELS GENERA

Petaurista, Pteromys, Glaucomys, Hylopetes, etc.

TRICKSTERS IN THE TREES

THE ACROBATIC AGILITY THAT MAKES THE ANTICS OF SQUIRRELS SUCH A DELIGHT TO WATCH IN THE WILD HAS ALSO HELPED MAKE THEM AMONG THE MOST SUCCESSFUL OF THE RODENTS

Few mammals have taken to the trees in such dramatic fashion as one rodent group—the squirrels. Whether in the conifer forests of the far north or in the equatorial rain forests, squirrels are among the most abundant of arboreal mammals. None can match them for the poise and seemingly effortless agility with which they traverse the treetops.

When ancestral squirrels became adapted for climbing—a time we have not yet pinpointed—a new and burgeoning food source lay at their disposal. While most other rodents scurried across the ground searching for edible items, the squirrels were able to pluck their food from the copious supplies on high, consuming seeds, nuts, fruit, and tender leaves as they emerged in the woodland canopy. They had to compete with birds, but their rodent teeth, built for gnawing, enabled them to break into hard seeds and nuts with relative ease and with an efficiency that few birds could match.

2109

Flying squirrels (below) *do not use powered flight, although they achieve a little lift from updrafts.*

S. Malowski/Frank Lane Picture Agency

Squirrels found a vacant niche and quickly made it their own. They spread rapidly in terms of distribution, abundance, and numbers of species. And as they continued to evolve, they became ever more adept at moving among the trees—climbing, racing along branches, leaping gaps, and even gliding from trunk to trunk.

Not all members of the squirrel family are tree-dwellers. The family also includes ground squirrels, such as marmots, chipmunks, and susliks. But the two groups considered in this volume—the tree squirrels and the flying squirrels—are true masters of arboreal life. Their bodies are ideally suited for such an existence.

TREE-BOUND TRAPEZE ARTISTS

The tree squirrels are the most familiar of the two groups. Abundant, active by day, very bold and inquisitive, and often taking to the ground, these are the squirrels well known as woodland dwellers in most parts of the world. In shape and habits they are highly distinctive. All have lithe, cylindrical, flexible bodies and strong limbs, and most have long, bushy tails—aids to climbing and balancing. Long toes equipped with sharp claws enable them to grip bark so firmly that, with their hind feet neatly flexed backward, they can hold themselves head-down even on vertical trunks. Moments spent motionless in gravity-defying postures are characteristic of tree squirrels.

L. Lee Rue/Bruce Coleman Ltd.

Tree squirrels have excellent senses of hearing and smell, and a finely tuned sense of touch, aided by sensitive whiskers not only on their cheeks, but also on their legs and feet. But it is perhaps their eyesight that is most remarkable. Their eyes are large and their vision acute, enabling them to negotiate their way across a tangle of twigs and branches while running at breakneck speed and to judge distances for leaping with pinpoint accuracy.

They are also among the few mammals that possess good color vision. This helps explain why tree squirrels tend to have more colorful coats than most

---

THE FUR OF TREE SQUIRRELS TENDS TO BE THICK AND SOFT, AND MANY SPECIES GROW PRONOUNCED TUFTS ON THEIR EARS

---

other rodents. Though some are predominantly gray or brown, others have richer colors or contrasting patterns of stripes. Coloration is most pronounced in some tropical Asian squirrels, especially the beautiful squirrels and the giant squirrels, which may have fur of red, pink, yellow, white, or black.

Despite the strong similarities throughout the group, tree squirrels do exhibit marked variations from species to species, not just in coloration but also in build, habits, and habitats. The size extremes in the group are especially striking. The Malabar giant squirrel of India weighs well over 100 times as much as the mouse-sized African pygmy squirrel.

GLIDERS OF THE FORESTS

Tree squirrels readily leap across gaps from tree to tree. The second group, the flying squirrels, have taken such ability a stage further. These nocturnal animals have evolved pronounced flaps of skin that extend between their limbs on either flank. When a flying squirrel is clambering over a tree trunk or branch, these folds are drawn tightly against the body so as to be inconspicuous. But when the squirrel leaps and stretches its limbs out, the flaps turn into a taut gliding membrane that enables the animal to sail for some distance to another tree.

Though less numerous in species terms and less well known than the tree squirrels, flying squirrels are widely distributed and often abundant in the forests in which they make their homes. Their gliding membranes aside, they share many of the physical features possessed by tree squirrels, including a narrow, supple body; long tail; flexible hind feet; sharp, curved claws; large eyes and ears; and thick fur. In size, they range from the

The gray squirrel holds a nut in its fingers,

maneuvering the food against its stubby thumbs.

mouse-sized pygmy flying squirrels of Southeast Asia to the cat-sized giant flying squirrels that are widespread in south and east Asia.

As already noted, no definitive statements can be made concerning the evolutionary origins of squirrels. The fossil evidence is too scant. The latest findings, however, do suggest that the precursors of today's squirrel family emerged in Asia some time during the late Paleocene epoch (55 million years ago) and quickly spread through the continent. By about 40 million years ago, there were ancestral tree squirrels and flying squirrels present in Europe. After the start of the Miocene epoch, some 27 million years ago, squirrels spread into North America and Africa.

SQUIRREL HEARTLANDS

Today, the tropical forests of Asia and the Indonesian archipelago remain the true heartland of the family. Half of all the species of tree squirrels and about three-quarters of the flying squirrels are found in this region. This rich environment yields a wealth of ecological niches for species to exploit. Although squirrels reached them fairly late, the tropical forests and woodlands of Africa and Latin America are also rich in species. The mix of squirrel species is fewer in the temperate and northern forests of North America, although the species that do occur in them, like the gray squirrel and the fox squirrel, are abundant and well known. But it is the northern forests of Eurasia that are poorest in species. Though the region is close to the squirrel heartland, Ice Age glaciation has made the forests poor in tree flora, with a more limited range of food sources to exploit. Only two species are native to the entire forest zone of Europe and northern Asia: the Russian flying squirrel and the red squirrel. ■

THE SQUIRRELS' FAMILY TREE

The squirrel family is grouped with several other rodent families under the category of squirrel-like rodents. This group probably diverged early on to form, among others, today's beavers, pocket gophers, and the true squirrels. Three main squirrel types have evolved from the ancestral true squirrel stock: the ground squirrels, the tree squirrels, and the flying squirrels. The flying squirrels are sometimes placed in a subfamily of their own.

Nick Pike/WLAA

GIANT FLYING SQUIRREL

Petaurista petaurista
(pet-ow-RIS-tah pet-ow-RIS-tah)

Flying squirrels differ from the other two groups in two main ways. They are nocturnal, and they possess membranes on their flanks for gliding between the trees. The 14 genera, which contain 37 species, **include the Old World flying squirrels, genus Pteromys; the New World flying squirrels, genus Glaucomys; and the giant flying squirrels, genus Petaurista, of Southeast Asia (illustrated above).**

SPRINGHARE

SCALY-TAILED SQUIRRELS

POCKET MICE

RED SQUIRREL

Sciurus vulgaris
(skee-YOUR-uss vul-GAR-iss)

The tree squirrels form the largest group among the squirrels, with over 130 species in 26 genera. All are arboreal, with slender bodies, rounded heads, large eyes, and long tails. They include the tree squirrels, genus Sciurus; the pine squirrels, or American red squirrels, genus Tamiasciurus; the giant squirrels, genus Ratufa; and the beautiful squirrels, genus Callosciurus. The red squirrel, shown here, is one of the most widespread species.

Nick Pike/WLAA

GROUND SQUIRREL

Spermophilus
(sper-moe-FILL-uss)

There are 10 genera, consisting of about 100 species, of ground squirrels. They include the marmots, genus Marmota; chipmunks, genus Eutamias; prairie dogs, genus Cynomys; and susliks, genus Spermophilus.

Though some climb into trees, ground squirrels are mainly terrestrial and burrowing animals, inhabiting various terrains. Their bodies tend to be stouter and their tails shorter than tree squirrels.

Kim Thompson

SQUIRRELS (SCIURIDAE)

BEAVER

MOUNTAIN BEAVER

POCKET GOPHER

B/W illustrations Ruth Grewcock

SQUIRREL-LIKE RODENTS

ANATOMY: THE RED SQUIRREL

SIZE COMPARISON
The red squirrel (above left) can reach 8.7 in (22 cm) from nose to rump, with a tail up to 7 in (18 cm) long and a maximum weight of 11.3 oz (320 g). The black giant squirrel (above right) of Southeast Asia may grow to 18 in (45.7 cm) from nose to rump, with a tail as long as its body or even longer. This giant can weigh up to 6.5 lb (3 kg).

THE LONG WHISKERS
enhance the sense of touch around the head. Further touch-sensitive bristles grow from the feet, the outside of the forelegs, and the underside.

THE EYES
are large, giving the red squirrel wide, accurate vision for judging distances in the branches. A high density of cones in the retina also give the squirrel good perception of color.

GIANT FLYING SQUIRREL
Hearing is a vital sense for flying squirrels, since they are active in the inky darkness of the forest at night and need to detect the approach of any nocturnal predators as soon as possible.

GRAY SQUIRREL
The ears of the gray squirrel lack the conspicuous tufts of the red squirrel, but they are equally sensitive to sounds of danger and of communication. Squirrels use a wide range of calls to signal one another.

THE FORELIMBS
are used to manipulate objects while it sits on its haunches.

The skeleton of the red squirrel reveals the light, flexible frame that enables the animal to move so easily in the trees. The hind limbs, which are larger than the forelimbs, give the animal most of the propulsion required when running or climbing. The long tail is an excellent balancing aid.

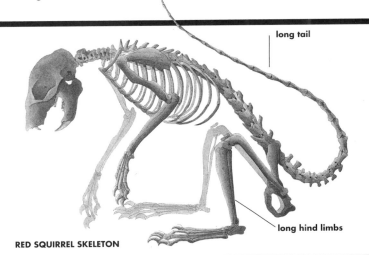

long tail

long hind limbs

RED SQUIRREL SKELETON

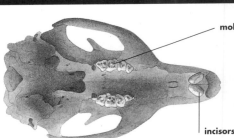

molars

incisors

RED SQUIRREL'S SKULL
As with all rodents, the rootless incisors grow continually and must be worn down to prevent excessive length. The molars possess roots.

X-ray illustrations Elisabeth Smith

FACT FILE:

THE RED SQUIRREL

CLASSIFICATION

GENUS: *SCIURUS*

SPECIES: *VULGARIS*

SIZE

HEAD–BODY LENGTH: 8–8.7 IN (205–220 MM)

TAIL LENGTH: 6.7–7 IN (170–180 MM)

WEIGHT: 9–11.3 OZ (250–320 G)

WEIGHT AT BIRTH: 0.3-0.4 OZ (8–12 G)

COLORATION

VARIES FROM BRIGHT, REDDISH BROWN TO DARK, GRAYISH BROWN OR ALMOST BLACK. IN WINTER, THE REDDISH FORM BECOMES DARKER AND GRAYER. UNDERSIDE IS PALE

FEATURES

LARGE, DARK EYES

PROMINENT EAR TUFTS

ROUNDED HEAD

THICK, BUSHY TAIL HELD UPRIGHT WHEN SITTING

LONG FACIAL WHISKERS

THE TAIL

is more than extravagant decoration. It can serve as a balancing rod when the animal is leaping or perching on a thin branch. It is also used like a flag to make complex signals to other squirrels, and it can function alternatively as a muffler or a sunshade in uncomfortable weather.

THE FUR

is soft and particularly dense in winter. The coat is deep reddish-brown above, with a creamy-white underbelly. The thin tail is chestnut to creamy white. The body fur is molted twice each year, in spring and autumn. The ear tufts and tail molt only once each year.

SHARP CLAWS

on the squirrel's feet allow it to hold fast to precariously sloping surfaces. The ankle joints are so flexible that the animal can rotate its hind feet backward to provide better support when descending a tree trunk.

SKULL

The squirrel has a fairly generalized skull for a rodent, with a rounded shape and simple teeth. When the animal is gnawing, the lower jaw is pulled forward by a muscle called the later masseter anchored in front of the eye. The scaly-tailed squirrel has a deeper, shorter skull, with much smaller projections of bone behind the eye socket.

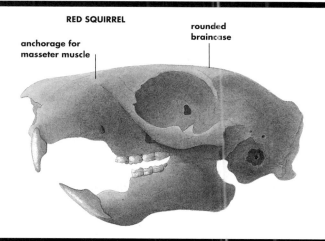

RED SQUIRREL

anchorage for masseter muscle

rounded braincase

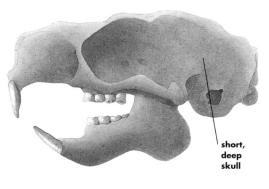

SCALY-TAILED SQUIRREL

short, deep skull

Main illustration Steve Kingston

HIGH-RISE HOMES

PLACES TO FEED, REST, BREED, AND FLEE FROM DANGER, TREES PROVIDE ALL THAT SQUIRRELS NEED FOR SURVIVAL, AND THE ARBOREAL LIFESTYLE MOLDS THE RODENTS' BEHAVIOR

Squirrels the world over are intimately associated with trees. The trunks, branches, and leafy canopies are the stages on which the animals play out their lives. This is where they make their homes, find most of their food, mate, and bring up their young. This is where they are in their element and feel secure.

Tree squirrels regularly descend to the ground to forage—flying squirrels do so much less—but they are always ready to race back to a nearby trunk as soon as any danger threatens. Simply taking up position at the base of a trunk may be enough if the danger is not imminent, for tree squirrels seem to be naturally bold and inquisitive creatures. They are, for example, unusually tolerant of human presence and may take cover from an approaching person simply by scuttling around to the opposite side of a trunk and regularly peeping out to see if all is safe. If unnerved, however, they will take rapidly to the canopy and bolt into a leafy refuge.

HOP, SKIP, AND JUMP

Tree squirrels, in general, are active during the day, especially in the periods after dawn and before dusk. They are busy foragers, moving rapidly about in the branches with their characteristic stop-and-start motion. When scampering at high speed along a branch, the animal holds its tail out behind as a balancing aid. The same aid is gained when perching on a delicate branch by shifting the tail from side to side as a counterbalance. If the squirrel needs to cross a short gap to the next tree top, it can make flying leaps to a new perch with its body flattened, legs spread, and tail extended to provide extra stability in the air. If the gap between trees is too great, however, the squirrel may have to cross via the woodland floor. Tree squirrels always descend trunks headfirst, gripping tenaciously with their

pin-sharp claws. Across the ground they move with graceful bounds, which are often punctuated by pauses when they check for danger. Should menace arise, they can break into a swift run.

FLY-BY-NIGHT

Flying squirrels, of course, have a more economical and more spectacular method of crossing large gaps between trees—one that also avoids ground predators. By stretching out their remarkable skin

Joanne van Gruisen/Ardea

The agility with which squirrels descend trees is displayed by this hoary-bellied squirrel (above).

The tail and limbs provide a squirrel with stability when it leaps between branches.

flaps, they turn leaps into glides. Small species, such as the southern flying squirrel of North America, can sail for up to 165 ft (50 m) from tree to tree. Giant flying squirrels can make flights of well over 330 ft (100 m), sometimes utilizing natural updrafts to gain extra lift. Since the motion is not powered, flying squirrels lose height as they glide, but they do nevertheless make a brief upward movement just at the end of the flight when they swing their body forward to meet the trunk feet first.

When not gliding, flying squirrels forage in the canopy with remarkable agility. If in danger when it lands on a tree, a flying squirrel can dash in moments up to a higher position, ready to take off again. But the slight impedance the furled membranes do present seems just enough to make daytime activity too risky. Probably to avoid attack by sharp-sighted birds of prey, flying squirrels are active at night. This still leaves them vulnerable to owls and nocturnal mammals, such as martens, and it has been observed that, on landing from a glide, some flying squirrels scurry at once to the far side of the tree trunk. Such evasive action thwarts any owl that might be swooping down behind them.

When the sun comes up, flying squirrels seek cover. Most find refuge in hollow trees or in the abandoned tree holes of woodpeckers. Some shelter in abandoned buildings. Tree squirrels may also den in hollow trees, filling cavities with dry vegetation and bedding down in it at night with their tails curled around their bodies for warmth. More often, however, species like the gray squirrel will build a nest in the tree canopy (see Habitats). ∎

The rare Malabar giant squirrel of India (above) grows to over 3 feet (about 1 m) from head to tail.

HABITATS

ZEFA

Between them, tree squirrels and flying squirrels have a distribution that spans most of five continents; they are absent only from southernmost South America, Australasia, and the oceanic islands. In the more arid habitats of tropical and temperate zones, their place is taken by ground squirrels.

Most squirrel species are highly dependent on woodland and forest habitats of various types. Across the world, they occur in dense, coniferous forest; mixed and deciduous woodland; open, heathy woods and dry woodland savanna; seasonal monsoon forests; and tropical rain forests. The fullness of the canopy and the lushness of the foliage differ considerably among these habitats, but they are all places where trees predominate, providing the food and shelter the animals require.

Some squirrel species are rather particular about the type of habitat they require. The Russian flying squirrel, for example, prefers conifer forests with tall trees, usually of spruce or pine. It keeps to the treetops so much that, given its nocturnal habits, it is seldom seen even in areas where it is common. The four species of neotropical dwarf squirrels prefer hill forests up to cloud level, in which palm trees are abundant. Palm fruits and nuts are their favorite foods.

THE AMERICAN RED SQUIRREL IS ALSO CALLED THE PINE SQUIRREL BECAUSE OF ITS FONDNESS FOR PINE WOODS

In some cases where closely related squirrel species overlap in range, it is noteworthy that they do not overlap in habitat. Among the Asiatic striped palm squirrels of India, there are species that prefer tropical forest and jungle, while others inhabit open palm woodland and scrubland. Two species of sun squirrels occur in West Africa—one is limited to rain forest, the other dwells in woodland savanna. Sometimes the differences are quite subtle: In the eastern broad-leaved woodlands of North America, for example, gray squirrels tend to inhabit the denser parts, while fox squirrels prefer the more open areas.

Squirrels also have a reputation for being adaptable and opportunist. Many are adept at finding what they need in a variety of habitat types. The red squirrel is often regarded as an animal of coniferous forests, but it can be equally at home in mixed and broad-leaved woodland. Some squirrels readily colonize man-made habitats, such as forest

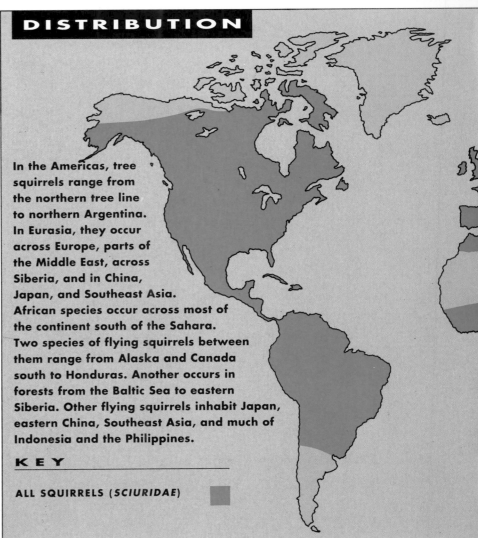

DISTRIBUTION

In the Americas, tree squirrels range from the northern tree line to northern Argentina. In Eurasia, they occur across Europe, parts of the Middle East, across Siberia, and in China, Japan, and Southeast Asia. African species occur across most of the continent south of the Sahara. Two species of flying squirrels between them range from Alaska and Canada south to Honduras. Another occurs in forests from the Baltic Sea to eastern Siberia. Other flying squirrels inhabit Japan, eastern China, Southeast Asia, and much of Indonesia and the Philippines.

KEY

ALL SQUIRRELS (*SCIURIDAE*)

Chasing is a key element of social behavior among tree squirrels. Individuals readily pursue one another around trunks, often in territorial disputes or pre-mating scuffles (left). These scrambles, which are a delight to watch, are accompanied by loud chatters and barks.

KEY FACTS

● The front incisor teeth of squirrels grow continuously to compensate for the wearing down caused by gnawing. The cheek teeth used for chewing are, by contrast, rooted.

● The little-known woolly flying squirrel of Kashmir is an unusual creature. It apparently lives in cold, rocky, open terrain at very high altitudes, where it probably feeds largely on mosses and lichens.

● One of the arrow-tailed flying squirrels, a group of squirrels that live in Southeast Asia, is said to nest sometimes in hollowed-out coconut shells still suspended in palm trees.

● A giant squirrel can make leaps between branches of 20 feet (6 m) or more, but this pales against the longest recorded glide of a giant flying squirrel, which stands at over 1,450 feet (450 meters).

● Occasionally young squirrels are forced to disperse large distances once they have left the nest. One juvenile fox squirrel migrated 40 miles (64 km) from its natal area.

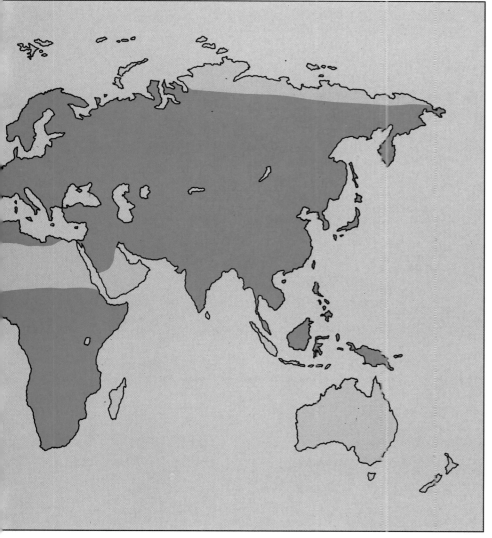

clearings, plantations, and areas of thick cultivation. The gray squirrel, when it was introduced into Britain from North America, spread rapidly not only through lowland wooded habitats, but it also very successfully colonized leafy English suburbs and city parks. Indeed, gray squirrels in London's Hyde Park and Regent's Park are so at ease in their urban surroundings that they will take food from people's hands. Some species among the beautiful squirrels of Asia have also moved into cultivated areas and suburbs.

In tropical and subtropical regions, forests covering the lower slopes of mountains provide lush habitats that are markedly cooler than the lowland forests. Several kinds of squirrels have become specialized for these forests, which for much of the time are shrouded in clouds. The five species of red-cheeked squirrels, genus *Dremomys*, inhabit montane forests in Asia; and the giant flying squirrels generally live in forests above 3,000 ft (900 m) in altitude, with some Himalayan species ranging as high as 13,200 ft (4,000 m). Given the rocky terrain on which many of the trees grow, it is not suprising that giant flying squirrels have been observed perching on vegetated cliffs.

Other squirrels have a closer association with rocks. The complex-toothed flying squirrel of China actually nests in cliff crevices and cavities, while the groove-toothed squirrel of Borneo forages mainly on the ground and often takes refuge among rocks. The largely ground-dwelling Berdmore's palm squirrel of Southeast Asia is one of the few tree squirrels that does not actually need trees: In parts of its range it lives among rocky shrubs.

Giant flying squirrels are known to make brief springtime migrations to lower altitudes to feed on early fresh growth of vegetation. In more northerly habitats, the season that brings about the most change in behavior is winter. Unlike many mammals of northern climes, squirrels do not hibernate, but they react to the cold weather by spending much more time in the nest or drey.

WARM AND DRY IN THE DREY

Perched on a fork of a branch or even on an old crow's nest, the drey is a hollow ball or dome of sticks, bark, and leaves lined with softer material such as dried grass, moss, and feathers. A squirrel will typically build several alternative nests for resting and refuge from predators, although one is usually a favorite. Females build maternity dreys in the breeding season, where their young spend the first weeks of life.

In midwinter, a red squirrel may leave its cozy drey to forage for only two hours per day. A thick winter coat grown after the autumn molt provides insulation, along with extra fat reserves that also

FOCUS ON

THE SCOTCH PINEWOOD

The ancient pinewoods of Scotland are among the remaining strongholds of the red squirrel in Britain. Having retreated from its former woodland haunts across most of the island, the red squirrel finds welcome refuge in these majestic wildwoods. Yet the natural pinewoods too have undergone a drastic decline. A few centuries ago they blanketed most of the Highlands, forming the vast Caledonian Forest. But land clearance and logging have reduced the forest to scattered remnants in remote valleys.

The natural pinewoods are dominated by Scotch pine—Britain's only native pine tree. A mature Scotch pine, with its fissured, rusty-red bark and unruly, flattened crown, may rise 100 ft (30 m) or more into the air. In some of the woods, the pines crowd close together, creating a shady, closed forest; elsewhere, the woods are more open and roomy. Scattered among the pines may be silver birches; and beneath the taller trees, rowan, aspen, yew, and juniper claim their spaces. In the clearings lie carpets of purple heather, bilberry, and bracken. The Scotch pines provide food and shelter for the red squirrel. The animal builds its drey within the evergreen crown of the tree, and pine seeds are its principal source of nourishment.

TEMPERATURE AND RAINFALL

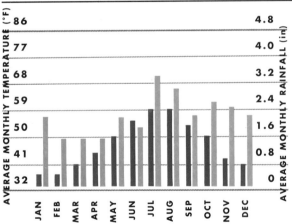

TEMPERATURE

RAINFALL

In the mild, moist summer, the pinewood is alive with floral color, birdsong, and the hum of insects. In the winter, gales blow and snow lies thick, but the red squirrel continues to forage in all but the worst weather.

help keep the animal going when food is hard to come by. In very cold or stormy weather, tree squirrels will remain in the shelter of the nest for up to several days until hunger forces them to emerge and look for buried food stores that they had set aside in the autumn. In particularly hard autumns, red squirrels have been known to make mass migrations to richer feeding grounds. A few tree squirrels may share the same drey to combine their warmth, and as many as twenty flying squirrels have been found huddling in the same winter nest. ■

NEIGHBORS

The clearings and shaded glades of the pinewood offer shelter and food to mammals, insects, and birds, many of which depend exclusively upon the rich harvest of cones and needles.

RED DEER

In high summer, newborn spotted fawns lie low and still in the heather while the adult red deer browse.

CAPERCAILLIE

This huge gamebird forages among the heather for berries, pine needles, shoots, insects, and spiders.

Illustrations A. Robinson/Wildlife Art Agency

ENEMIES

SCOTCH PINEWOODS

Relics of the ancient Caledonian Forest survive in pockets of Scotland, particularly in the west and in the valleys of the Dee and Spey in the east. Their total area of some 20,000 acres (8,000 hectares) is far exceeded by the area of land under commercial pine plantations.

■ **PINEWOOD**

PINE MARTEN
This mustelid pursues red squirrels, racing and leaping along branches with almost as much agility as its prey.

LONG-EARED OWL
This owl is robust enough to snatch squirrels from the trees at dusk, tracking them mainly by sound.

EXTREMELY DANGEROUS

MODERATELY DANGEROUS

M. Danegger/HHPA

PINE BEAUTY MOTH	CROSSBILL	WOOD ANT	SISKIN	EYED LADYBUG

The striped green-and-white caterpillars of the pine beauty moth feed on pine needles.

The crossbill's twisted beak is ideal for clipping out the seeds from the scales of pinecones.

Wood ants construct piles of pine needles over their subterranean nests on the pinewood forest floor.

The agile siskin is typical of the Scotch pinewoods, where it lives year-round. This finch feeds on pine seeds.

Larger than most ladybugs, this species and its larvae hunt devotedly for pine-needle aphids.

FOOD AND FEEDING

Robert Maier/Aquila Photographics Ltd.

Tree squirrels and flying squirrels are best known as consumers of nuts and seeds—food sources that are both abundant and highly nutritious. Many nuts that people eat are also a feast for squirrels, among them hazelnuts, chestnuts, walnuts, and hickory nuts. But whereas humans employ nutcrackers to reach the kernels, the squirrel uses its powerful rodent teeth. Holding the nut firmly in its paws and upper incisor teeth, the squirrel gnaws a hole in the shell with its lower incisors and then inserts these teeth to lever and crack the shell open. With this masterful technique, a squirrel can break open a hazelnut in a few seconds. The seeds of pinecones are extracted from the hard scales that contain them with similar efficiency.

Squirrels also supplement their diet with a wide variety of other food items, including fruit, berries, leaves, shoots, buds, bark, sap, and fungi. In a number of tropical-forest species, these sources are actually more important than seeds and nuts. The Malabar giant squirrel, for example, is quite dependent on fruit, while giant flying squirrels feed heavily on young leaves. The Sunda tree squirrels of Southeast Asia are especially fond of tree sap. Many squirrels also feed opportunistically on

insects and other invertebrates and even, on occasion, small vertebrates, such as tiny lizards and snakes, young birds, and birds' eggs. The long-nosed squirrel of Southeast Asia is an insect-eating specialist. It hunts on the ground and uses its peculiar elongated snout to probe for and snatch up ants, termites, beetles, and worms.

FOOD CACHES

Each squirrel typically has a few favorite feeding sites—places where the animal takes food it has gathered to eat in safety. Usually the site is high in a tree near the base of a branch, but it may also be on an old tree stump. Always the site provides good all-around views, so that the squirrel can detect the approach of danger while it feeds. The ground beneath the site is often littered with nut and cone debris, testament to the squirrel's copious appetite. A red squirrel may strip its way through an average of well over 100 pinecones per day, or some 40,000 in a year, accounting for a yearly consumption of no fewer than two million seeds!

In the seasonal forests of northern latitudes, nuts tend to be produced in crops, usually in autumn. Squirrels then find themselves surrounded by a

Two red squirrels eating (above). They are both using their forepaws to hold the food and their sharp teeth to chisel into it. The tails are used as a balance while they perch.

BURIED TREASURE

Like many squirrels, the gray squirrel buries small stores of food when sources are plentiful. It will later search for its hidden caches by sniffing carefully over the ground.

(in)SIGHT

BARK-STRIPPERS

The gray squirrel has a notorius habit shared by several other squirrel species—a habit that has made it unpopular with foresters. At times, the animal strips patches of bark from living trees. The tough outer bark is of no interest to the squirrel, but the sweet sapwood beneath is a source of food. This contains the tree's circulatory system, and it is through vessels in the sapwood that the tree transports water and minerals up from its roots and sugars and proteins down from its leaves. Wounds caused by gnawing squirrels damage the tree's growth and spoil the standing timber. Worse still, if the squirrel girdles the tree (strips bark all the way around the trunk), it may block the tree's circulation completely, leading to its death. Squirrels tend to attack young trees only a few decades old because their bark is easier to remove; the slender girth of these trees also increases the chance they may be girdled. Squirrels also tend to gnaw on the best, most vigorously growing specimens—the trees that have the thickest, most nutritious sap tissue.

Liz & Tony Bomford/Ardea

superabundance of their favorite food. Faced with a supply that exceeds their daily requirements, tree squirrels and flying squirrels seem to have an innate tendency to make small stores, or caches, of food. Nuts and cones are buried in the ground or hidden in tree holes and fallen logs. In winter, when conditions are harsh, a squirrel will search for caches using its sense of smell to check out likely places. A squirrel does not appear to memorize the location of its hoards, but it will take steps to prevent the seeds from sprouting by nipping out the seed germ or by burying cones in dry sites to prevent germination. ■

Illustration R. M. Budden/Wildlife Art Agency

SOCIAL STRUCTURE

The social lives of tree squirrels and flying squirrels are played out, like other aspects of their behavior, mostly in the trees. This is where they meet, mate, communicate, chase, and fight.

LIVING ALONE

Squirrels, for the most part, do not form lasting pair-bonds and are not gregarious creatures. Both sexes are promiscuous and separate after mating, and each animal spends most of its life alone within its home range. But there are exceptions to the rules. Both giant squirrels and giant flying squirrels have been observed in pairs, and most squirrel species are known to congregate in certain situations. One male gray squirrel was observed bringing his mate food because her pregnancy made her too fat to fit through the hole in the "squirrel house." Squirrels will also share nests during harsh weather.

This last fact underlines the finding that, though solitary in habit, most squirrels are not strictly territorial. Each occupies a defined home range, but the boundaries are not defended exclusively and the home ranges of males, in particular, frequently overlap those of their neighbors. A single home range may overlap with as many as six others, and

Leonard Lee Rue/Bruce Coleman Ltd.

TREETOP HOME
The favorite site for the gray squirrel's drey is the open treetop, where it is often seen perched in the fork of branches.

A gray squirrel (left) emerges from its tree hole. Like flying squirrels, tree squirrels will also make their dens in tree hollows, filling them with dry vegetation and other material to provide comfort and warmth.

ⓘⓃ SIGHT

THE ART OF GLIDING

Though a flying squirrel does not have the advantage of powered flight, it glides through the forest air with wonderful grace and precision. From high in one tree, it first sizes up the range to its target tree and then pushes off into space. Immediately it stretches out its legs and tail, pulling its gliding membrane, or patagium, into action. The patagium extends from the neck to the wrists, back to the ankles, and in some species around to the base of the tail. Thin rods of cartilage projecting from the wrists act like struts to support the leading edge of the membrane.

Nick Bergkessel/Oxford Scientific Films

INSIDE THE DREY

Constructed from sticks, bark, and leaves, the drey is lined with grass, moss, and feathers.

it is not uncommon for four neighboring squirrels to share the use of the same woodland spot.

Again, however, there are exceptions. Pine squirrels, or chickarees, agressively defend exclusive territories in the boreal and mountain forests of North America. Each territory is usually centered on a good supply of pinecones to which the owner tries to maintain sole access. In winter, pine squirrels also defend food caches in the territory, each of which may contain hundreds of cones. Intruders are met with loud, rattling calls, followed by darting chases up and down trees and through the branches. To establish a new territory even in a vacant site can take several hours of determined display and chasing against the owners of bordering territories.

Typical home range sizes vary considerably from species to species and between the sexes. In the broad-leaved woods of the eastern United States, gray squirrels may occupy permanent home ranges as small as 1.25 acres (0.5 hectares), while the fox squirrel often forages over 17.5 acres (7 ha). The home ranges of male gray squirrels are up to twice as large as those of females, and often overlap with them—a feature common to a number of squirrel species.

SQUIRREL-SPEAK

Squirrels use a range of signals to indicate their presence in a home range. Marking of prominent spots and pathways by gnawing bark and roots and by depositing urine, feces, and glandular secretions leaves long-lasting signs. These are reinforced by calls and display postures. Squirrels chuckle, chatter, bark, snort, and squeal and flash visual signals by moving their tails, pale bellies, ears, and eyelids.

But communication between squirrels involves

Illustration R. M. Budden/Wildlife Art Agency

much more than merely advertising their presence. Scent marks, calls, and visual cues are like a social information service, indicating local population changes and food availability, conveying individuals' breeding conditions, and their readiness to allow others to approach. The information exchange can be very precise. Squirrels typically utter warning calls when danger threatens, which serve to alert their neighbors. A recent study of three species of beautiful squirrels in Malaysia revealed that markedly different calls are made depending on the type of predator detected. A terrestrial carnivore will elicit repeated staccato barks that tell any squirrel listening to run up into the trees. A

LIVING IN HARMONY

For the tropical tree squirrels listed below, sharing a habitat does not pose a problem. Lifestyle and diet sufficiently set the species apart.

DAY

UPPER LAYER

PREVOST'S SQUIRREL

BLACK GIANT SQUIRREL

CREAM GIANT SQUIRREL

MIDDLE LAYER

BLACK-BANDED SQUIRREL

HORSE-TAILED SQUIRREL

PLANTAIN SQUIRREL

UNDERSTORY

LOW'S SQUIRREL

PYGMY SQUIRREL

FOREST FLOOR

THREE-STRIPED GROUND SQUIRREL

TUFTED GROUND SQUIRREL

SLENDER SQUIRREL

SOFT FRUIT/NUTS   LEAVES   INSECTS   BARK AND SAP

Illustration R. M. Budden/Wildlife Art Agency

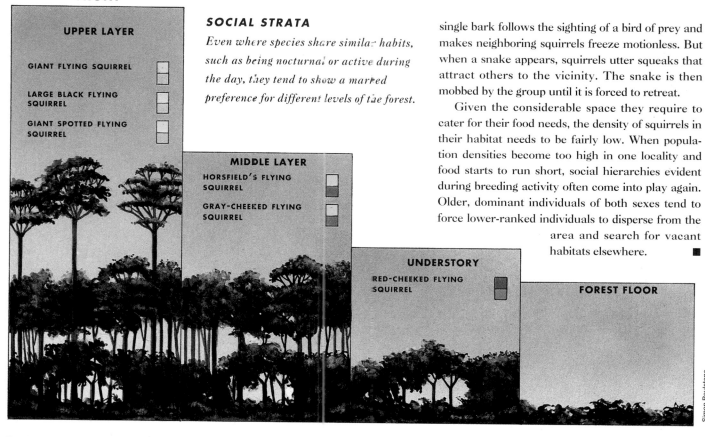

NIGHT

UPPER LAYER

GIANT FLYING SQUIRREL

LARGE BLACK FLYING SQUIRREL

GIANT SPOTTED FLYING SQUIRREL

MIDDLE LAYER

HORSFIELD'S FLYING SQUIRREL

GRAY-CHEEKED FLYING SQUIRREL

UNDERSTORY

RED-CHEEKED FLYING SQUIRREL

FOREST FLOOR

SOFT FRUIT/NUTS　　LEAVES　　INSECTS　　BARK AND SAP

Simon Roulstone

SOCIAL STRATA

Even where species share similar habits, such as being nocturnal or active during the day, they tend to show a marked preference for different levels of the forest.

single bark follows the sighting of a bird of prey and makes neighboring squirrels freeze motionless. But when a snake appears, squirrels utter squeaks that attract others to the vicinity. The snake is then mobbed by the group until it is forced to retreat.

Given the considerable space they require to cater for their food needs, the density of squirrels in their habitat needs to be fairly low. When population densities become too high in one locality and food starts to run short, social hierarchies evident during breeding activity often come into play again. Older, dominant individuals of both sexes tend to force lower-ranked individuals to disperse from the area and search for vacant habitats elsewhere. ■

FELLOW GLIDERS

HANGING AROUND

Flying lemurs spend the day hanging from branches or within tree holes in their rain-forest homes, the patagium folded around their bodies like a cloak. Unlike flying squirrels, they cannot fully withdraw the patagium, so they are not as agile when climbing.

Flying squirrels do not occur in Africa, but their place is taken there by another group of rodents, the scaly-tailed squirrels. Scaly-tailed squirrels are remarkably similar in appearance and habits to flying squirrels, yet they are not closely related. In fact, the seven species in three genera form a separate family, called the Anomaluridae, from the true squirrels. The similarities appear to be the result of animals' adapting in the same way to a similar environment.

Scaly-tailed squirrels inhabit the dense, tropical forests of Africa, where, just like flying squirrels, they keep largely to the treetops, shelter among foliage or in tree holes, feed on vegetable matter, and are mostly active at night. They climb trunks and scurry through the branches with speed and agility, and, most remarkably, possess an almost identical gliding membrane that extends from the neck to

the wrists and ankles and to the base of the tail. One obvious difference between the two sets of animals, however, is the feature from which the scaly-tailed squirrels take their name. Prominent overlapping scales near the base of the tail appear to give the animals extra grip on bark when landing and climbing.

The flying lemurs of Southeast Asia, Indonesia, and the Philippines provide another example of evolutionary convergence on the gliding habit. These animals are not even rodents—they belong to the order Dermoptera—yet they too possess a gliding membrane attached to the neck, limbs, and tail. The patagium of a flying lemur *(far left)* is the most extensive flight membrane of any mammal, running from the tips of the webbed toes and claws, all the way back to the tip of the tail. When gliding, this cat-sized animal looks like a kite.

LIFE CYCLE

The timing of breeding in most squirrels is geared to the availability of food. Some tropical rain-forest squirrels can breed at any time of the year; but even in this comparatively nonseasonal environment, most species have their breeding peaks during the periods when certain key foods—especially fruit—are most abundant. In northern latitudes reproduction is concentrated in early spring and summer, when warmth and plentiful food is assured, though mild winters can trigger breeding too.

The breeding behavior of temperate tree squirrels has been most closely studied, but observations of other species' habits indicate that they have much in common. Male squirrels, and in some species female squirrels, tend to be promiscuous. During the breeding season, a female coming into estrus will soon attract a group of males from the vicinity that follow her as she moves around in her home range. Casual following turns into more vigorous mating chases, with as many as ten males vying to keep as close as possible to the female. In

LIFE IN THE NEST

Nourished by their mother's milk, infant squirrels develop fast. After a few weeks the young are covered in fur and their teeth start to develop. And from about six weeks they start the switch to solid food. Once they have reached independence, they try to establish space for themselves in the neighborhood, but the unlucky ones have to face the perils of dispersing farther afield.

Liz & Tony Bomford/Ardea

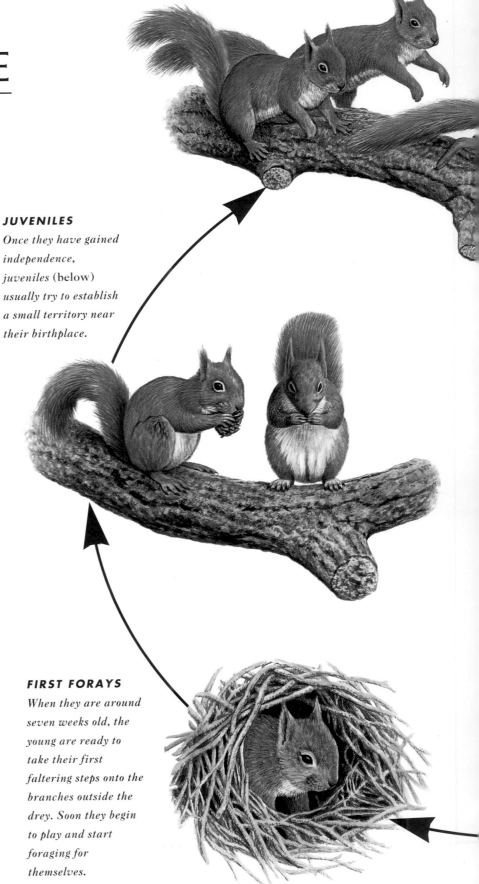

JUVENILES

Once they have gained independence, juveniles (below) usually try to establish a small territory near their birthplace.

FIRST FORAYS

When they are around seven weeks old, the young are ready to take their first faltering steps onto the branches outside the drey. Soon they begin to play and start foraging for themselves.

GROWING UP

The life of a young red squirrel

most cases it is the dominant males that accompany her most closely. At this time, she takes pains to keep the males a modest 3.3–6.6 ft (1–2 m) away, but when she is ready for mating she lets the closest approach with little courtship ritual.

In the gray squirrel, the males gradually disperse after one has mated—including the successful male, who rarely takes a further role in the rearing of his offspring. But in some squirrels, among them species of beautiful squirrels, the female may mate with a succession of up to six males in a mating bout lasting an entire morning.

After mating, the female prepares her nursery drey and the males retire either back to their home ranges or to pursue another female in the vicinity. After three to six weeks, depending on species, the female gives birth to a litter of naked, helpless young. A red squirrel litter usually contains several young, while that of a giant squirrel consists of just one or two. But the latter may compensate for this by producing multiple litters during the year, while the red squirrel manages at best two. ∎

Illustrations Simon Turvey/Wildlife Art Agency

COURTSHIP

When a female red squirrel is ready for mating (usually twice a year), males will gather around her and chase her until one of them is allowed to mate.

NEST-BUILDING

After mating, the female prepares a nest for her young, lined with soft plant material. She becomes very protective of her nest-tree, driving any intruding squirrels away.

HELPLESS LITTER

A litter of young is born in the drey after some thirty-eight days. The tiny pink infants emerge naked and helpless, with no teeth and their eyes and ears closed.

FROM BIRTH TO DEATH

RED SQUIRREL

BREEDING: USUALLY 2 SEASONS SPANNING JANUARY–MARCH & MAY–JULY
GESTATION: 38 DAYS
LITTER SIZE: 3–8
NUMBER OF LITTERS: 1 OR 2 PER YEAR
WEIGHT AT BIRTH: 0.3–0.4 oz (8–12 G)
EYES OPEN: 3 WEEKS
WEANING: 8 WEEKS
SEXUAL MATURITY: 11 MONTHS
LONGEVITY: USUALLY 2–3 YEARS, BUT UP TO 5

SOUTHERN FLYING SQUIRREL

BREEDING: USUALLY 2 SEASONS SPANNING FEBRUARY–MAY & JULY–SEPTEMBER
GESTATION: 40 DAYS
LITTER SIZE: 1–6
NUMBER OF LITTERS: 1 OR 2 PER YEAR
WEIGHT AT BIRTH: 0.07–0.1 oz (2–3 G)
EYES OPEN: 3 WEEKS
WEANING: 8–9 WEEKS
SEXUAL MATURITY: 9 MONTHS
LONGEVITY: NOT KNOWN

FEELING THE SQUEEZE

THOUGH A FEW SQUIRRELS HAVE BEEN BUSILY EXPANDING THEIR RANGES WITH HUMAN HELP, OTHERS HAVE SUFFERED FROM HUNTING, HABITAT LOSS, AND UNWELCOME COMPETITION

S quirrels, like so many wild animals, have had to cope with tremendous pressures as the human population that shares their world has steadily expanded: pressures directed particularly at them and pressures that are simply the by-product of increasing human settlement.

HUNTED BY HUMANS

Direct pressures have come from exterminators and hunters. The antics and cute appearance of squirrels endear them to people the world over, but squirrels' habits have sometimes brought them into conflict with humanity. Tree squirrels can cause extensive damage to young forestry trees by girdling them and chewing shoots, and they sometimes attack agricultural crops such as corn. Damage caused to lodgepole pines and other softwoods by native pine squirrels can be a serious problem in commercial plantations in North America. In Britain, the relentless spread of the nonnative gray squirrel over the last 100 years has caused an animal, initially introduced for aesthetic pleasure, to become a serious woodland and forest pest. In places where there has been serious damage to timber and crops, people have used a battery of weapons—traps, poisons, and shotguns—to bring squirrel numbers down.

Guns and traps have also long been used by squirrel hunters. The United States is one country in which squirrels are extensively shot as game animals. Giant flying squirrels are killed in some parts of their range as a source of meat. But hunting for fur and other squirrel parts also has a long tradition. In the cold forests of Siberia, for example, the Russian flying squirrel and the red squirrel grow thick, high-quality fur, and their pelts have been a

valuable export commodity since the Middle Ages. European expansion into the the boreal forests of North America established a large-scale fur trade there, too, focusing on the pine squirrels. All these species are still hunted for their fur—the Canadian pine squirrel trade was recently worth an estimated one million dollars annually. Gray squirrels have also been hunted for their tail hairs, which are used in artists' brushes that are sometimes advertised as

Habitat loss due to forest clearance is threatening the future of many squirrel populations (right).

Martin Wendler/Oxford Scientific Films

A red squirrel hangs in a hunter's trap. In some regions its pelt is still a prized trophy.

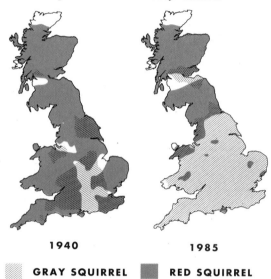

THEN & NOW

This map shows how the gray squirrel increased its range between 1940 and 1985, while that of the red squirrel was drastically reduced.

1940   **1985**

GRAY SQUIRREL   RED SQUIRREL

From being widespread across all of Britain at the start of the century, the red squirrel has gradually disappeared from all but a handful of locations in central and southern England and is dwindling alarmingly in Wales, northern England, and lowland Scotland. Simultaneously, the gray squirrel, which was repeatedly introduced into Britain from 1876 to 1930, has expanded its range. The match between the red's decline and the gray's advance was so close that it soon became clear that the alien squirrel was replacing the native species. Gray squirrels are very adaptable in diet, habitat, and the degree of disturbance they tolerate. Released into Britain, they have flourished in broad-leaved woodlands not dissimilar from the woods of their native North America.

being made of camel's hair. Native people of Borneo have traditionally used the bushy tail of the groove-toothed squirrel to decorate the sheaths of large knives called parangs.

LOSING THEIR HOMES

Indirect pressures on tree squirrels and flying squirrels have resulted from the loss and modification of their natural habitats. While hunting has generally not had too much impact on the overall populations of squirrels, habitat change most certainly has. Forest clearance to make way for farms, roads, settlements, plantations, neighborhoods, and other forms of land development has

David Woodfall/NHPA

SQUIRRELS IN DANGER

THE CHART BELOW SHOWS HOW THE INTERNATIONAL UNION FOR THE CONSERVATION OF NATURE (IUCN), OR THE WORLD CONSERVATION UNION, CLASSIFIES THE FOLLOWING SPECIES OF TREE AND FLYING SQUIRRELS:

DELMARVA FOX SQUIRREL	ENDANGERED
MOUNT GRAHAM RED SQUIRREL	ENDANGERED
DANGS GIANT SQUIRREL	ENDANGERED
MAHARASHTRA GIANT SQUIRREL	ENDANGERED
CAROLINA FLYING SQUIRREL	ENDANGERED
VIRGINIA FLYING SQUIRREL	ENDANGERED
AFRICAN PYGMY SQUIRREL	VULNERABLE
CARRUTHER'S MOUNTAIN SQUIRREL	VULNERABLE

ENDANGERED MEANS THAT THE ANIMAL IS IN DANGER OF EXTINCTION AND ITS SURVIVAL IS UNLIKELY UNLESS STEPS ARE TAKEN TO SAVE IT. *VULNERABLE* MEANS THAT IT IS LIKELY TO BECOME ENDANGERED IF PRESENT CIRCUMSTANCES CONTINUE.

destroyed the habitats of countless squirrels. Even where forests remain, alterations to the habitat brought about by tree-felling, woodcutting, the planting of exotic trees, and other actions can harm some squirrel species by reducing their food supply, making the canopy too thin to travel through, or removing potential nesting sites.

The red squirrel's decline in Britain, though hastened by the introduction of gray squirrels, had been taking place long before. Red squirrels need extensive woodland stretches with closely spaced trees so that they can leap easily from one crown to the next. Centuries of woodland clearance have not only removed large areas of habitat,

A gray squirrel being hand-fed in Regent's Park, London. Appealing though its antics may be, in some regions this squirrel would be viewed as a pest and hunted accordingly.

but also have fragmented and thinned much of the rest, making it unsuitable for the native species. Clearance of big, old trees with plenty of holes has caused the Russian flying squirrel to decline in the west of its range, and similar problems endanger populations of the northern flying squirrel in the states of Virginia and North Carolina.

Deforestation throughout the tropical and subtropical regions threatens, or is likely to threaten, numerous squirrel species, especially those dependent on intact primary rain forest. Among the list of those vulnerable to decline are Peter's squirrel of central Mexico, the African palm squirrel, the African pygmy squirrel, and several races of giant squirrels and arrow-tailed squirrels in south and east Asia.

GRAVE THREATS

Some squirrels with restricted ranges face particularly grave threats. Logging in its isolated upland forest home has helped reduce the population of the Mount Graham red squirrel of Arizona to just 150 individuals. This race of the pine squirrel is therefore at risk of extinction if any further disturbance is made to its habitat. A race of the fox squirrel now confined to the Delmarva Peninsula of the eastern United States has already become extinct over most of its former range and survives in only a few scattered locations.

Interestingly, the fox squirrel has expanded its range in some other areas, most notably in the old prairie lands in the central and midwestern states, where tree-planting and farming have created potential habitats and food supplies where few previously existed. ∎

ALONGSIDE MAN

PETS AND FOLKLORE

The image of the squirrel as inquisitive and enchanting has reappeared in history from ancient myth, through fairytales to a host of modern children's stories. They have featured in folklore and, almost wherever they occur, have been popular for centuries. Red squirrels were kept as pets as long ago as Roman times. Large numbers of Asian beautiful squirrels are still caught for the pet trade.

Excavations in an old graveyard in Hungary have revealed the remains of children accompanied by squirrel skeletons—presumably the children's pets sent with them into the afterlife.

Joe G. Blossom/Survival Anglia

INTO THE FUTURE

Peter Bull/Wildlife Art Agency

The key to preserving endangered and restricted species of tree squirrels and flying squirrels is to conserve as much of their preferred habitat in as pristine a state as possible. For tropical-forest species, in particular, this means not just maintaining large tracts of uncleared forest but also preventing the selective removal of the large trees favored both by loggers and by canopy-dwelling squirrels.

For those declining temperate woodland species whose natural habitat has already been heavily modified, conservation may need to involve more active habitat management and restoration to create homes most suitable for the squirrel in question. For canopy-loving squirrels, it is important to protect large nut- or mast-producing trees and also to encourage the crowns to grow wide, perhaps by removing some intervening trees or thinning the forest. Removing exotic trees rather than native

PREDICTION

UNCERTAIN FUTURE

Continued deforestation is likely to put further species of tree squirrels and flying squirrels under threat, particularly in the tropical regions. Elsewhere, conservation efforts are likely to prevent isolated species from dying out completely.

trees is preferable, since the latter are more likely to provide a food supply for the native squirrel.

When replanting or restoring an old woodland habitat designed to support squirrels, it is usually best to plant a variety of native trees so that the animals have different sources of food to fall back on should one type fail. Sometimes the best habitat for a squirrel is not dense woodland; the fox squirrel, for example, thrives best in open, parklike woods.

Red squirrels in Britain have their most secure strongholds in Scotch pinewoods, but they have also been helped in upland England and Wales by the creation of extensive conifer plantations. Management of suitable coniferous habitats is probably the only way red squirrels can survive now in Britain since the eradication of gray squirrels is not feasible. To enhance their prospects, foresters can avoid clear-cutting large areas, ensure that plantation trees reach cone-bearing age before they are cut, and maintain a mixture of conifer species and ages to maximize their food and shelter value for red squirrels. ∎

MANAGEMENT DILEMMA

Maintaining exclusive habitats for the red squirrel poses something of a dilemma for British conservationists. Gray squirrels cannot manage on a diet of solely pine seeds, but they can feed on them in conjunction with broad-leaved seeds and nuts and other foods. Therefore any conifer forest or plantation that has even a quarter mix or less of other trees is likely to be invaded by gray squirrels. To keep the squirrels contained, conservationists would have to remove most broad-leaved trees from within and around the refuge.

Ironically, conifer plantations in Britain have been criticized for their lack of tree diversity, making them poor habitats for wildlife overall. Attempts have been made to improve their habitat value by encouraging shrubs and planting patches of broad-leaved trees, but this in turn has opened the door to gray squirrels. To create new refuges for red squirrels, conservationists may therefore have to implement some unpopular forms of habitat management.

HOME HELP

Nest boxes placed strategically on tree trunks have been shown to double the population of squirrels in areas where there is plenty of food and cover but too few secure nest sites. Nest boxes are particularly useful for the hole-nesting flying squirrels, and they have been used to try to help the recovery of the Virginia flying squirrel, whose population currently stands at only 250 individuals.

Nest boxes are starting to be employed to boost the survival of red squirrels in Britain. In areas where reds share their habitat with gray squirrels, the latter can be prevented from taking over the boxes by making the entrance holes just 2 in (5 cm) wide—big enough for red squirrels to enter but too narrow for the larger grays.

TASMANIAN DEVILS

RELATIONS

The marsupial carnivores, family Dasyuridae, belong to the order Marsupialia, which also includes:

KANGAROOS

KOALA

POSSUMS

WOMBATS

Alan Root/Okapia/Oxford Scientific Films

CLASSIFICATION

The Tasmanian devil the largest living member of about fifty species of pouched meat-eaters called marsupial carnivores that form the superfami Dasyuromorphia. Most are with the dev in the family Dasyuridae. There ar three other families, each with one species.

ORDER

Marsupialia
(marsupials or pouched mammals

SUBORDER

Polyprodontia
(bandicoots, marsup carnivores, and American opossums

SUPERFAMILY

Dasyuromorphia
(marsupial carnivore

FAMILY

Dasyuridae
(cat-, rat-, and mous like forms)

TASMANIAN DEVIL

GENUS

Sarcophilus

SPECIES

harrisii

DEVIL IN DISGUISE

NAMED FOR ITS BLOODCURDLING GROWL AND SUPPOSED FIERCE
HUNTING HABITS, THE TASMANIAN DEVIL IS REALLY A QUIET
CARRION FEEDER THAT CAN EVEN BE TAMED AS A FRIENDLY PET

It is a quiet night in the patchy forest and bushland of Tasmania, Australia's southernmost state. The peace is broken only by the rustle of leaves and the shrill *more-pork* call of the boobook owl. Suddenly the stillness is shattered by a deep, menacing growl that increases in volume and becomes a penetrating whine, and then rises to a piercing screech. It sounds as though the Devil himself is abroad in the bush. This is the call of a Tasmanian devil, angry at being challenged by another of its kind for the night's meal of a dead wallaby.

The Tasmanian or native devil is about the size of a medium-sized dog, but it has the proportions of a small bear—with a longer tail. It is a marsupial, or pouched mammal, and the largest surviving member of the group called the marsupial carnivores. The Tasmanian devil got its name partly from its growling, whining call, which sounds much too loud for this relatively small, compact creature. It was also supposed to be a bloodthirsty killer of sheep, poultry, and other livestock. This was in the early days of European settlement in Tasmania, in the 19th century. But it is now known that the "devil" is fairly peaceable, although, like most wild animals, it can be fierce

UNLIKE THE MOUSE-SIZED KILLERS TO WHICH IT IS RELATED, THE DEVIL MAKES FOR A FAIRLY FEEBLE PREDATOR

and angry when provoked. And while it does kill for food occasionally, it is chiefly a scavenger, munching and crunching the dead bodies of animals ranging from wallabies to mice. It is said that the Tasmanian devil has trouble killing a rat and is itself easily killed by a dog.

THE MARSUPIAL CARNIVORES

The devil is the largest of about fifty-five species of marsupial carnivores, sometimes known by their biological name of *dasyures*. Most dasyures are small and look like stoats, rats, mice, or an odd combination of the three; the devil itself is unusually stocky and squat for its kind. The smallest is the long-tailed planigale, a pointy-snouted, mouselike inhabitant of the dry, cracked, clay soils of inland

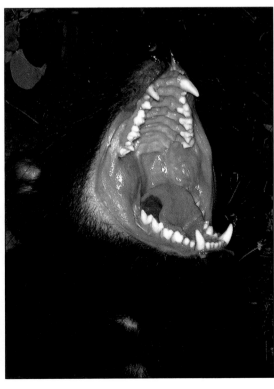

Jean-Paul Ferrero/Ardea

Few animals need cower at this sight; the devil's jaws are used mainly for crushing carrion (above).

DASYURES VERSUS OTHER MARSUPIALS

A. G. Wells/Oxford Scientific Films

Fat-tailed dunnart babies suckle from their mother's teats (above).

Like other marsupials, a female dasyure nurtures her tiny young in her pouch until they develop. But the pouches of some dasyures are mere flaps of skin, rather than deep bags, and they open toward the tail, never forward as in kangaroos. The phascogales lack a pouch altogether. The babies simply seize the mother's nipples with their mouths and nestle in her belly fur, gripping with their toes.

eastern Australia. It weighs only 0.14 oz (4 g), making it the smallest of all marsupials—and one of the world's smallest mammals.

Their outward resemblance to cats, rats, or mice led early European settlers to christen many of the dasyures with common names such as "marsupial mouse" or "marsupial rat." The settlers, however, knew little of the lifestyle of these unfamiliar creatures; "marsupial weasels and shrews" might be more apt. For the dasyures are far from being seed-eaters like mice and rats; they are almost all fierce hunters that prey on other animals for food.

Many of the marsupial carnivores also have names of Aboriginal origin. In addition, some of them—such as the antechinuses and planigales—are known by Latin scientific names that have passed

A western native cat (left) *investigates a branch, sniffing for food with its supersensitive nose.*

A. G. Wells/Oxford Scientific Films

ANATOMY:
THE TASMANIAN DEVIL

The Tasmanian devil is knee-high to a human when standing fully erect, with about the same body size as a cocker spaniel. The thylacine, now assumed to be extinct, was 5 ft (1.5 m) from nose to tail. The smallest marsupial carnivores, such as the narrow-nosed planigale, have a head-and-body size barely greater than a man's thumb.

Barry Croucher/Wildlife Art Agency

THE SNOUT

is long, with plenty of sensitive whiskers for feeling the way in the dark, and well-developed olfactory organs inside for the keen sense of smell.

THE EYES

are small and beady, not large like many night-active animals, since the devil chiefly uses its sense of smell to locate food and assess its surroundings.

JAWS
The jaws gape widely. Powerful muscles give a terrific biting force to crunch up gristle and bones.

four incisors each side

UPPER JAW DENTITION

Most marsupial carnivores have four pairs of upper incisors and three pairs of lower incisors. Some have five upper pairs. The canine teeth are long and pointed, as in many carnivores, for stabbing and tearing the meaty meal. The cheek teeth are large and ridged, for shearing gristle and cracking bone.

cheek teeth

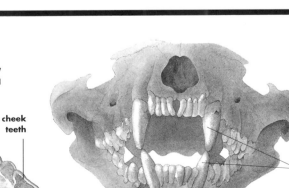

The head is large in proportion to the body, to accommodate the heavily built jaws, large teeth, and highly developed jaw muscles.

large canines

X-ray illustrations Elisabeth Smith

THE FUR

is smooth and black and covers most of the devil's body. Sparse hair on the snout and the insides of the ears allows the pink flesh to show through.

THE TAIL

may be lifted up or swished back and forth when the devil is agitated, alarmed, or afraid. This happens mainly when it defends its meal against a challenger of its own kind.

FACT FILE:
THE TASMANIAN DEVIL

CLASSIFICATION

GENUS: *SARCOPHILUS*

SPECIES: *HARRISII*

SIZE

HEAD-BODY LENGTH/MALE: 23.5-30 IN (60-76 CM)

HEAD-BODY LENGTH/FEMALE: 20-25 IN (51-64 CM)

TAIL LENGTH/MALE: 10-12 IN (25-30 CM)

TAIL LENGTH/FEMALE: 8-10 IN (20-25 CM)

WEIGHT/MALE: USUALLY 15-20 LB (7-9 KG)

WEIGHT/FEMALE: 11-15 LB (5-7 KG)

COLORATION

BACKGROUND COLOR: BLACK OR ALMOST BLACK

MARKINGS: MOST DEVILS HAVE A WHITE PATCH OR "COLLAR" ON THE THROAT OR NECK, AND PERHAPS WHITE PATCHES ON THE REAR SHOULDERS, RUMP, AND POSSIBLY TAIL TIP; ALL-BLACK DEVILS ALSO OCCUR

FEATURES

SMALL, BEADY EYES

SQUAT, STOCKY BUILD, LIKE A SMALL BEAR

TAIL UP TO ONE-HALF OF BODY LENGTH

The five-toed forefeet do not have especially large claws, but the devil is a competent climber, can dig well, and can manipulate food with the forepaws.

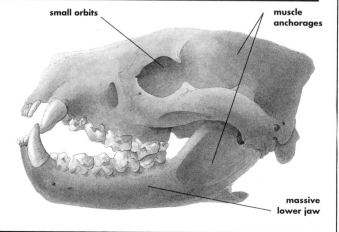

small orbits

muscle anchorages

massive lower jaw

extensive pads

curved claws

ADAPTABLE LITTLE DEVIL

AFTER A POPULATION CRISIS EARLIER THIS CENTURY, THE TASMANIAN DEVIL HAS SPREAD TO MANY DIFFERENT HABITATS. BUT MOST OF ITS FELLOW MARSUPIAL CARNIVORES HAVE BEEN FAR LESS FORTUNATE

Lacking larger native enemies to prey upon it, the devil has little to fear in its island home of Tasmania. So it trots about the forest and bush at night, largely undisturbed. Much of its night is taken up by scenting the air for the smell of fresh blood or rotting meat and following the scent to its source.

The devil is a solitary animal, and each has its home range. It is not territorial, however, so does not patrol or mark its borders, defend any area, or chase away intruders. The occasional meeting is usually marked only by a mutual, wary sniff. Only when several devils try to commandeer the same carcass do squabbles tend to break out.

Dawn sees the devil retiring to a safe den to rest and sleep, remaining mostly unnoticed by the day shift of hunters and hunted. It may rouse itself to groom, drink, or defecate, and then return to sleep until dusk. Provided there are no disturbances by its former main enemy—humans—the devil lives a relatively peaceful life.

SMALL BUT FIERCE

This unruffled existence is in sharp contrast to most of the devil's smaller dasyure cousins. Some of the tiny antechinuses and dunnarts, in particular, may look cute, but they are fierce predators. For food, they must tackle other mammals, lizards, and insects, which are almost as large as themselves.

If threatened by a larger predator, these tiny dynamos usually dash away into a small crack or under a log, where the bigger animal cannot follow. But if cornered, they do not hesitate to hurl themselves at the predator in a flurry of scratching claws and gnashing teeth, following the strategy that counterattack is the best form of defense.

Many marsupial carnivores live in the dry, red, rocky Australian outback. To avoid the searing heat of the day, and to prevent water loss through panting

or perspiring to keep cool, they sleep in cracks in the soil or under rocks or fallen branches. Some of the dasyures have preferred daytime refuges. The Pilbara ningaui, small as a shrew, takes shelter in the dense, capacious hummocks of spinifex. This is a type of tussock grass that grows along drainage lines in the rocks in its restricted range of the Hammersley Plateau, Western Australia.

During the day, some dasyures may become active, but only for short periods. Usually they wake up, groom their fur, clean their paws and whiskers, and perhaps venture a short distance from the refuge or nest to defecate.

ANT/NHPA

A female eastern quoll (above) *rears up to sniff out a meal of carrion.*

Three-month-old dusky antechinuses (below) *curl up tight in their underground nesting chamber.*

Andrew Henley/Biofotos

As the sun sets, the marsupial carnivores emerge and begin their search for prey. Some species, like the devil, have tracks that they follow on a regular basis. Others, like the planigales, wander mainly at random, following any sound or scent that might indicate a meal. This nocturnal lifestyle is a common strategy among desert animals, and some regions of desert are consequently much more active at night compared to the daytime. Because many of their prey animals are nocturnal for survival reasons, the marsupial carnivores have adopted a similar lifestyle for feeding as well as survival.

EXTRA DEEP SLEEP

Some of the smaller dasyures undergo a short-term, halfway version of hibernation called torpor. The stripe-faced dunnart is one example. This shrewlike marsupial lives across huge tracts of central Australia, although nowhere is it common. For a few hours while it sleeps, the dunnart's body temperature may drop by several degrees. Its heartbeat and breathing rate slow down, also.

By slowing down body processes, torpor helps the dunnart to save energy. It is especially effective in very small mammals, which have a large body surface relative to their body volume and so lose heat rapidly compared to larger mammals. The extra heat must come from food, which is why little mammals such as bats and shrews seem always to be eating. ■

For such a small, secretive mammal, the devil is surprisingly vocal (left).

ZEFA

HABITATS

The Tasmanian devil favors coastal scrublands and sclerophyll forests with rocky outcrops, found mainly in the northern half of Tasmania. Sclerophyll forest consists mainly of trees with leathery leaves to reduce water loss because of low rainfall or rocky, fast-draining soils. The forest trees and rocky outcrops provide fallen logs, or cracks and caves, where the devil can rest by day.

In the past few decades, the devil has spread into other habitats, partly due to the availability of food. Sick or dying livestock, especially sheep, are an easy meal for a carrion-feeder, as are wallabies and other animals that have been killed on roads. In addition, various grubs, beetles, and other plant pests have spread as a result of agriculture, and the devil is not above eating these morsels as small but tasty midnight snacks.

As a result, the devil has taken to living in bushy scrub, wasteland, farmland, parkland, and even the outer suburbs of towns. It sometimes uses dens under old outbuildings. It is now widespread across most of Tasmania, except for parts of the south. However, the hilly, rocky, wooded country of the interior is still its main stronghold.

DISTRIBUTION

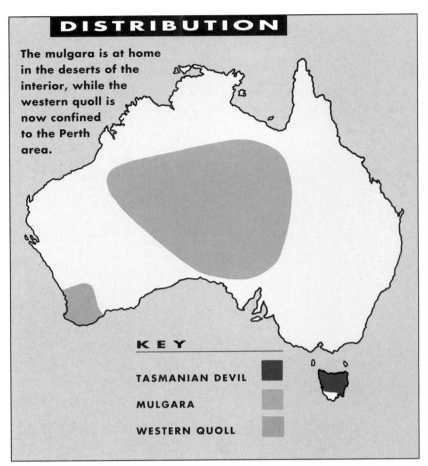

The mulgara is at home in the deserts of the interior, while the western quoll is now confined to the Perth area.

KEY

TASMANIAN DEVIL

MULGARA

WESTERN QUOLL

ANT/NHPA

AUSTRALIA'S SOLE BURROWER

Although a few of Australia's mammals will readily take to a hole in the ground, one alone is truly adapted for a burrowing lifestyle. The marsupial mole, *Notoryctes typhlops,* is a living drill bit. It has a toughened forehead and rigid vertebrae to help it thrust through the soil, and its shortened limbs are armed with huge, flat claws. It even lacks functional eyes and ears. It lives in the central deserts where, unusually for a burrower, it does not make permanent tunnels but allows the sand to collapse behind it as it progresses.

Hans & Judy Beste/Ardea

Tasmania may look insignificant on a map when compared with mainland Australia, but with an area of 26,250 sq mi (68,000 sq km), it is a little larger than West Virginia—with a comparatively tiny population. And compared with countries such as Great Britain, large areas of Tasmania are still very rural and unspoiled. They make fine wilderness areas.

FOREST NEIGHBORS

The Tasmanian devil shares some of its habitats with the much more secretive eastern native cat (*Dasyurus viverrinus*). This stoatlike, white-spotted dasyure was once common around southeastern Australia but has disappeared from most parts of the mainland. This has occurred despite its ability to adapt to sclerophyll forest, heathland, scrub, and farmland. The disappearance may be due to a disease epidemic at the turn of the century, coupled with competition from introduced cats and foxes.

The devil's range is also home to larger animals such as kangaroos and wallabies, the widespread brush-tailed possum, the common wombat, the brown bandicoot, and other marsupials. In addition, the hilly, rocky forests support various bats, owls, and hawks and other birds of prey, snakes such as the copperhead, and lizards such as the fence skink. The locally famous Tasmanian cave spider inhabits damp, sheltered cracks and corners, from caves to

Kathie Atkinson/Oxford Scientific Films

Two young common planigales (above) *at play. Tiny but fierce, they will pick on prey as big as themselves*

The fat-tailed dunnart (left) *is usually solitary, but in cold conditions it will huddle with others to keep warm.*

old logs or road drains. Almost all of these neighbors may be eaten by the devil when they die.

The northern native cat, or satanellus (*Satanellus hallucatus*), has also adapted well to human habitation. It is the smallest of the four quoll species and prefers the warmth of the tropics. It is fairly widespread along the northern coastal districts, from Western Australia across the Northern Territories to Cape York Peninsula and down Queensland to Townsville. Within this range it can occupy most habitats, from dry, rocky countryside with sparse vegetation to thicker woodland, and even around farms and outlying buildings.

KEY FACTS

● The Tasmanian devil is one of the few marsupial carnivores to hold its own since Europeans arrived in Australia.

● The devil has few natural enemies or competitors. This is partly because dingoes and introduced foxes have not spread from the Australian mainland across to Tasmania, and partly because the thylacine is now believed to be extinct.

● Some dasyures have been generally unaffected by the European settlements, chiefly because they inhabit the dry interior, which is unsuitable for pasture or crops.

● Another group of dasyures, such as the sandstone, cinnamon, and Atherton antechinuses, have an extremely limited range—in a few cases, down to less than ten square miles.

The habitats of certain other dasyures are also well known, but few are spreading their range. Most have become restricted since the European settlement of Australia began in the 19th century. One example is the western quoll, or native cat (*Dasyurus geoffroyi*). When the settlers arrived, it could be found in almost any place with scattered woodland and sclerophyll forest. This meant around most of the continent, from Esperance in the southwest in a clockwise direction all the way to Adelaide. The quoll was thought to be absent only from the southern coasts along the Great Australian Bight and from the dry interior.

Today, the western quoll is rare or absent from most of its former range. It is limited chiefly to the heavily forested southwest corner of Western Australia, from Perth across to Ravensthorpe. It hunts both in trees and on the ground, sneaking up silently on birds as they roost at night, as well as taking small mammals and reptiles such as lizards. It also consumes smaller prey, from insect grubs and larvae, such as caterpillars, to earthworms.

OUT IN THE OUTBACK

Fortunately, some dasyures have suffered little from the European invasion. This is because they are adapted to the harsh, dry habitat of Australia's

"red center"—a huge expanse of hot, dusty land that is of little use for grazing or plowing.

The rat-sized mulgara can survive in areas where the annual rainfall is 4 in (10 cm). It extracts all the moisture it needs from its diet of mice, birds, and beetles, and it hides in its cool burrow during the hottest hours of the day. Even in these most arid habitats, which stretch from Pilbara in Western Australia across to southwestern Queensland, the mulgara is still relatively common among the stones and scattered bunches of spinifex grass. ▪

FOCUS ON

CHEYNE BEACH

The coastal stretch of Cheyne Beach, near Albany, Western Australia, is the stronghold of the dibbler or freckled marsupial mouse. This tiny dasyure eats insects, worms, and other small invertebrates, and also nectar and pollen. When disturbed, it has been observed to dash and hide in leaf litter, where it also hunts for food.

The main flowers of Cheyne Beach are species of banksia with spiked or bottlebrush blooms. There are also thick swards of grass and scattered trees. Two of the very rare recorded captures of the dibbler were on flowers of *Banksia attenuata*.

Since the discovery in 1967 of dibblers in the area, further searches have found only a few specimens. The indications are that the dibbler occupies a tiny area in the extreme southwestern tip of Western Australia—one of the most restricted ranges of any marsupial.

There are now nature preserves to protect this extremely threatened marsupial around Cheyne Beach and Jerdacuttup. Since much of the habitat is, however, close to human settlements, marauding cats and foxes also present a threat.

TEMPERATURE AND RAINFALL

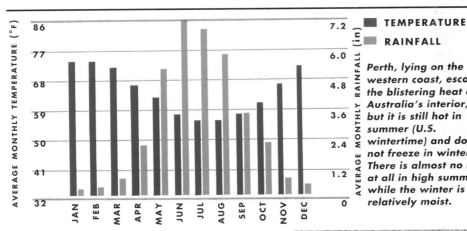

■ TEMPERATURE
■ RAINFALL

Perth, lying on the western coast, escapes the blistering heat of Australia's interior, but it is still hot in summer (U.S. wintertime) and does not freeze in winter. There is almost no rain at all in high summer, while the winter is relatively moist.

NEIGHBORS

Unlike neighboring New Zealand, Australia is rich in endemic (native) species. The grassy cover of Cheyne Beach is an ideal habitat for small marsupials.

BANDICOOT

The southern brown bandicoot nests on the ground in southern scrub, heath, and forest areas.

BOOBOOK OWL

This small hawk owl of Australia also lives in New Zealand and New Guinea.

Illustrations James Higgins/WLAA

CHEYNE BEACH AND THE ALBANY AREA

Cheyne Beach, near Albany, is some 220 mi (350 km) southeast of Perth. It lies on the southernmost point of Western Australia, although it is still several degrees latitude north of Tasmania.

• Perth

Cheyne Beach

ANT/D. Whitford/NHPA

BROWN GOSHAWK

Supremely agile, the goshawk preys on almost anything it can find.

COPPERHEAD SNAKE

The copperhead is one of Tasmania's two venomous snakes, although it is most common in Victoria.

GRAY BUTCHERBIRD

The sweet song of this thick-billed bird belies its grisly habit of impaling its insect prey on thorns.

KANGAROO

These familiar marsupials occupy most of Australia, including both Tasmania and the Albany area.

COMMON WOMBAT

Absent from most of the continent, this burrowing grazer is widespread throughout Tasmania.

FOOD AND FEEDING

Over the years, the devil has been accused by farmers of taking livestock, especially lambs and poultry, and of killing needlessly or "for pleasure." It is true that devils eat livestock and can become pests on farms. But their victims often turn out to be sickly or very old or young. Devils do get into poultry pens and kill the hens; they have also been seen eating lambs and other livestock. But their reputations as wanton killers are exaggerated.

The devil is basically a scavenger or carrion feeder. If hungry enough, it will eat almost anything of animal origin. Its teeth, jawbones, and jaw muscles are so strong that it can crush and consume the lot—skin, muscles, guts, and bones. The only leftovers are the hard teeth and large bones.

ANT/NHPA

The fat-tailed dunnart (left) earns its name from the fat reserves in its tail, which nourish it when food is scarce.

A HUNGRY DEVIL *makes short work of a freshly killed wombat (below).*

ONE RESEARCHER, WATCHING A CAPTIVE DEVIL EATING THE GUTS OF A DECEASED ANIMAL, LIKENED THE SPECTACLE TO "SOMEONE EATING SPAGHETTI"

Experiments in captivity showed that if a laboratory rat is put into the cage of a Tasmanian devil, the devil has great trouble killing it. If the rat fights back, the devil may become nervous and retire into the corner. The rat may even set up home and live as a cage mate, in an uneasy truce! However, once a devil has managed a kill, or found a carcass, feeding is meticulous. It often drags the prey to a secluded spot, where it tears off chunks of flesh and swallows them whole. It tears out the guts and stuffs them into its mouth with its forepaws. It licks up any spilled blood and crushes the bones with its jaws. Any bones or teeth too hard to tackle are gnawed and licked clean.

In the case of a large carcass, such as a forester kangaroo or Bennett's wallaby, several devils will gather to dig in. They feed together but tend to squabble over food. These loose feeding groups usually consist of local animals, who therefore tolerate each other. But if a stranger appears, it is

Illustration Rachel Lockwood/Wildlife Art Agency

PREY

The Tasmanian devil eats the remains of almost anything and everything it can find on its nocturnal wanderings. Birds, farm livestock, and even other marsupials are all devoured where available.

COMMON WOMBAT

CRAYFISH

DOMESTIC POULTRY

FROGLET

repelled aggressively. And if food is in short supply and the devils are hungry, then the atmosphere soon turns sour. To guard its share of the meal, the devil crouches low and utters low growls; the body rises, as does its voice; the jaws gape ever wider. The final challenge is a loud sneeze and then a jaw-wrestling contest. Finally one contestant backs down and retreats, and the winner glares after it.

The devil eats a bewildering range of carrion. It dines on small and soft meals such as worms and agricultural pests, right up to adult kangaroos. In between are wombats, possums, and potorcos, smaller mammals such as mice and rats, birds and their chicks, lizards and skinks and other reptiles, and the freshwater crayfish known as yabbies. And almost anything else! ■

THE MARSUPIAL TERMITE-EATER

George Bingham/Bruce Coleman Ltd.

The squirrel-sized numbat (*Myrmecobius fasciatus*) has the most specialized diet of the marsupial carnivores. It is nicknamed the marsupial or banded anteater, but by far its main food is termites, only rarely eating ants. Its rod-shaped, sticky tongue is half as long as its head and can be flicked out at astonishing speed to gather food.

The numbat does not usually try to work its way through the hard-baked mud wall of termite mounds, or break open the timber to reach nests inside old logs. Its front limbs and claws are not really powerful enough. Instead, it rakes out and exposes the termite runs—the shallow tunnels or galleries that radiate from the main nest—along which the termites travel.

The numbat has fifty to fifty-two small teeth—more than any other marsupial—but it rarely uses them for eating. It simply whips the termites into its mouth on the sticky tongue, then swallows them whole.

This rare species is now restricted to areas of western and perhaps southern Australia, having suffered from habitat destruction and predation by foxes. Its main habitat is eucalyptus woodland, where there is a regular supply of hollow logs and old wood for its tiny insect prey. In keeping with its unique lifestyle, it is also active only in the daytime, unlike the other nocturnal dasyures.

LAMB

SCRUB WREN

WALLABY

POSSUM

POTOROO

Prey illustrations Ruth Grewcock/Wildlife Art Agency

HUNTING

Unlike the Tasmanian devil, most marsupial carnivores attack their prey ferociously. Even the tiniest can kill and consume creatures almost as big as themselves. The Pilbara ningaui (*Ningaui timealeyi*) is little larger than your thumb, yet its prey includes poisonous desert centipedes and big, hard-cased cockroaches. The ningaui subdues them after a brief struggle and rips out the softer pieces of flesh with its tiny, pointed teeth. Captive ningauis also eat small skinks and frogs and insects such as crickets and grasshoppers, but they avoid millipedes and beetles.

Another small yet fierce mouse-shaped hunter is the long-tailed dunnart, *Sminthopsis longicaudata*. It lives in scattered locations across the rugged, rocky screes of the center and west of Western Australia. It is well named, since the tail is about 8 in (20 cm) long—over twice the length of its head and body. This dasyure has rarely been observed in the wild, but we know something of its feeding habits from analysis of its droppings. Victims include lots of beetles, ants, cockroaches, flies, grasshoppers, spiders, and centipedes.

The dusky antechinus (*Antechinus swainsonii*) is a forest-floor feeder. This shrewlike dasyure is restricted to Tasmania and the southeastern coast of mainland Australia, preferring hilly areas such as the Kosciusko National Park and the Brindabella Range, where the annual rainfall

THE AGILE *eastern quoll readily scales trees to raid birds' nests of their fledglings* (right).

The devil (above) *tends to shy away from live prey unless it finds sickly or old animals or infants that it can easily subdue.*

LOOKING LIKE *a larger replica of its marsupial mouse prey, a mulgara silently, patiently stalks its quarry. It will skin its prey neatly before eating it.*

Illustration Peter David Scott/Wildlife Art Agency

exceeds 40 in (100 cm). The dusky antechinus forages on the forest floor, digging with its strong legs and claws. It unearths a wide variety of small prey, such as worms, beetles, centipedes and millipedes, grubs, and larvae. It subdues each victim with bites, then picks it up in its forepaws and stuffs it into its mouth. This is one of several dasyures that supplements its diet with plant material, such as blackberries and other fruits. Another is the rare dibbler (see Cheyne Beach, page 2146), which may eat nectar and pollen from flowers and also the beetles, flies, and other insects that are likewise attracted by the nectar.

FAST AND FURIOUS

The rat-sized mulgara of arid central Australia is known for its lightning attacks on prey. It has been observed killing house mice at incredible speed. This endears it to humans as, several times, the house mouse has reached plague proportions since it accompanied European settlers to Australia.

When a mulgara sees a likely victim, it suddenly becomes still as a statue. Slowly, its body stiffens and tenses, and the tail may quiver. Then it leaps and springs, too fast for human eyes to follow, and seizes the back of the prey's neck in its jaws. It may bite there several times, dropping the victim in between. After a pause to lick itself clean, the mulgara starts at the head and works its way into the body of the victim, chewing the internal parts, and leaving the bones and skin as an empty bag. It eats about one-quarter of its body weight in flesh daily.

Andrew Henley/Biofotos

The spotted-tailed quoll or tiger cat, *Dasyurops maculatus*, is the biggest of the quolls and the second-largest dasyure. Accordingly, this secretive forest-dweller hunts bigger prey, and descriptions such as "the most combative creature of the Australian bush" are well founded. A fine climber, it takes roosting birds, as well as robbing their nests of eggs or chicks, and pounces on gliding possums in the branches. On the ground it preys on mice, rats, rabbits, and other mammals up to the size of small wallabies, as well as snakes and other reptiles, frogs, and insects. Like the devil, it scavenges the carcasses of sheep and other livestock. ∎

A dusky antechinus devours a spider that it has caught, handling it dexterously with its finely clawed forepaws. This dasyure also feeds on lizards, worms, and insects.

LIFE CYCLE

Most marsupial carnivores breed once a year, in winter or spring, although dunnarts produce two litters each year. The Tasmanian devil usually breeds at the end of its second year, although most other dasyures breed in their first year. The female devil produces two young in the first season, and three or four annually for the next three years or so. Dunnarts may produce twenty young each year.

In March, the female devil's pouch enlarges. By April, males and females pair up. The male keeps the female in his den for about two weeks before they mate. In some dasyures, copulation lasts several hours. The pair may stay together until the young are independent.

THE FEMALE PHASCOGALE WOULD SEEM
TO BE UNIMPRESSED BY COPULATION:
SHE IS LIKELY TO FALL ASLEEP
DURING THE ACT!

Most dasyures have a gestation of 21–28 days; in the dunnarts it is only 12 days. Gestation in the devil is 31 days, after which usually four young are born. They are each the size of a baked bean; only the forelimbs are well developed, with claws to crawl to the four teats in the pouch. The young devils stay attached to the teats until 13 weeks old. By this time they are furred and their eyes are open.

By late September the young have outgrown the pouch, so the adults build them a grass nursery nest in a sheltered spot. The male helps to defend the nest and brings food to his mate, but he ignores

IN LATE SPRING
the male and female come together to mate. It is an aggressive affair, but the male often assists the female for several months.

AT TWO YEARS
the devil is sexually mature; now it starts to seek out a mate.

Andrew Henley/Biofotos

The brown antechinus, like most dasyurids, is nocturnal. It spends the day resting in a nest, usually inside a hollow log (left).

GROWING UP

The life of a young devil

THE NAKED

newborns are tiny, with outsized heads. Having found a teat, they hang on tight for about three months.

FULLY FURRED

at fifteen weeks, with their eyes open, the young start to investigate their surroundings but remain safely under cover.

AT TWENTY WEEKS

the devil is fully weaned and capable of feeding on carrion.

Robin Budden/Wildlife Art Agency

FROM BIRTH TO DEATH

TASMANIAN DEVIL	COMMON DUNNART
GESTATION: 30–32 DAYS	**GESTATION:** 12–14 DAYS
LITTER SIZE: 3 OR 4	**LITTER SIZE:** UP TO 10
SIZE AT BIRTH: 0.4–0.6 IN (10–15 MM)	**SIZE AT BIRTH:** 0.2–0.3 IN (5–8 MM)
EYES OPEN: 10–13 WEEKS	**EYES OPEN:** 3–4 WEEKS
WEANED: 5 MONTHS	**WEANED:** 9 WEEKS
INDEPENDENT: 6 MONTHS	**INDEPENDENT:** NOT KNOWN
LONGEVITY: 7–8 YEARS	**LONGEVITY:** 1–2 YEARS

his offspring. The young stay and play at the nest while their mother forages. They are weaned after five months, but they continue to follow the mother, hanging on to her fur or heels, until November or December, when they become independent.

QUOLLS AND PHASCOGALES

Quolls mate between April and June; the gestation period is sixteen to twenty-one days. The female has only six teats, yet may give birth to up to thirty young. The babies are attached to the teats for seven weeks. They begin to leave her and start to play at thirteen weeks, and they are independent at eighteen weeks.

The phascogales also have a winter courtship. Like many dasyures, the female lacks a proper pouch, but has folds of skin around her eight teats, which enlarge during the thirty-day gestation period. More than eight young are born, so some die at once—a strange feature common to several species, including the quoll. The surviving youngsters stay attached to the teats for forty days, then the mother makes a nursery nest, where they are based until weaned at five months. The juveniles may stay in the nest until the next breeding season, when they are fully grown and sexually mature. ∎

AMAZING FACTS

DEATH FROM MATING

In many of the antechinuses, the male searches frantically for a suitable female. Competing males battle strenuously to win a mate. Mating, too, is action packed, taking twelve hours as the male bear-hugs the female and grips her neck in his teeth.

Stressed by searching for a mate, fighting off other males, and copulating endlessly, nearly all males die after mating. This means that hardly any male antechinuses live for more than one year. It also leaves the females and young with no local competition for food.

DEVIL'S ISLAND

THE DEVIL SEEMS TO BE HOLDING ITS OWN OUT ON TASMANIA, BUT SEVERAL OF ITS DASYURE COUSINS ARE IN TROUBLE. THE THYLACINE HAS ALREADY GONE MISSING, PRESUMED EXTINCT

The marsupial carnivores have a long history, having survived relatively peacefully before human settlers reached their island paradise. Earlier in their history there were marsupial hyenas, saber-toothed cats, bears, and lions. The large, flesh-eating marsupial lion, *Thylacoleo carnifex,* may have died out less than 30,000 years ago. Coincidentally, the first humans and wild dogs (dingoes) reached Australia perhaps 40,000 years ago.

TASMANIAN STRONGHOLD

The population of Tasmania is small, around half a million people. The island's area is a little larger than that of West Virginia. The number of people per unit area is one-third that of West Virginia—which is good news for the devil. There are large tracts of undisturbed wilderness, rocky and inaccessible—so inaccessible, in fact, that some people still hope that the largest marsupial carnivore, the thylacine (Tasmanian tiger or wolf), which has gone missing and is presumed extinct, may one day be rediscovered, living in the remote northeast or northwest of the state.

There have been many supposed sightings of the thylacine since the last known specimen was captured in 1933 and died in Hobart Zoo in 1936. The thylacine was a doglike hunter with powerful jaw and head muscles operating a mouth with an extraordinarily large gape. The stripes on the back gave it the name of tiger, although it was much more wolflike in general build. It also possessed the typical marsupial reproductive system.

The thylacine was once widespread on the mainland, but became extinct perhaps 2,000 years ago, probably in competition from the dingo, which never crossed the Bass Strait to Tasmania. The thylacine thrived on Tasmania until the Europeans arrived with their sheep—an ideal source of food for this "marsupial wolf." Conflict with farmers was perhaps inevitable. From the 1820s, bounties were offered for the scalps of thylacines, and these were eagerly accepted by hunters known as "doggers." In 1888, the Tasmanian government officially joined the hunt, offering rewards for thylacines, alive or dead. The species was becoming rare by 1900, but there seem to have been further reasons for the population crash around 1905–1915: This may have been an epidemic of disease. By the 1920s, the thylacine was on the way out. Ironically, the year that the last zoo individual died was the same year that the species was given official protection.

The Franklin-Lower Gordon Wild Rivers National Park in Tasmania (right).

ANT/NHPA

The last thylacine ever seen died in captivity over 60 years ago (above). *Today, it may be extinct.*

Jean-Paul Ferrero/Ardea

THEN & NOW

The map below shows the former and present distribution of the Tasmanian devil.

▨ **FORMER**   ■ **PRESENT**

Fossils and other remains of devils show that the species was once common on mainland Australia. The rich, fossil-bearing sediments of Wellington caves, New South Wales, have yielded remains about 15,000 years old of devils that are larger than today's versions and may belong to a separate, larger species. Most recent specimens are only a few hundred years old, after which time it seems that the devils died out on the mainland.

The Tasmanian devil has also been rare in the past. The same disease epidemic that affected the thylacine may explain the devil's scarcity around 1908–1910. On the mainland, the eastern quoll was similarly affected. Again in the 1950s, the Tasmanian devil became rare, but today its numbers have built up again and it is not considered to be in much danger. Indeed, devils have become pests in some areas, attacking poultry and young pets, and sometimes control measures are needed.

This cannot be said of other dasyures. They face several problems, one of the most serious being predation by, and competition from, introduced species. As predators, cats and foxes have devastated the populations of native wildlife in many parts of Australia. One researcher estimated that feral (gone-wild) cats kill 400 million native mammals, birds, and reptiles each year. The dasyures may not be the most common victims,

ENDANGERED SPECIES

since they are often able to fight back fiercely. The introduced carnivores have upset the general balance of wildlife by competition, too. They prey on small mice, birds, and other creatures that might otherwise feed the dasyures.

Rabbits, another introduced species, have also had far-reaching effects on Australian wildlife. Their nibbling has destroyed vast areas of natural vegetation, starving out the local small herbivores on which many marsupial carnivores feed.

The problem of introduced species is particularly severe in Australia, whose marsupials and other wildlife have long evolved in isolation. However, another major threat is faced by wild creatures the world over: habitat loss due to human activity. Natural landscapes have been transformed by many forces. One is the burning or clearing of native scrub and bush to make way for grazing land for cattle and sheep. Another is logging for timber, especially along the eastern side of the

> THE QUOLL HAS SUFFERED THROUGH PREYING ON THE HIGHLY VENOMOUS CANE TOAD, WHICH WAS INTRODUCED TO CONTROL CROP PESTS SUCH AS RATS

country, although many sites are now managed in a sustainable manner. Vast areas have been taken over in this way, driving out the local wildlife. Since much of the expansion took place in the last century and the first half of this century, the grazed pastures have become almost accepted by some people as the way things have always been.

COLLECTING DATA

Another problem in a land as vast as Australia lies in gathering enough accurate information. The fawn antechinus (*Antechinus bellus*) lives in the far north of the Northern Territory, in Arnhem Land to the west of Darwin. It is one of the largest of the antechinuses, with a head-and-body length of 5 in (13 cm) and a tail of 4 in (10 cm), and it looks like a rat.

Scientists long believed that the fawn antechinus was a rare creature, an isolated tropical cousin of the much more common yellow-footed antechinus. In the 1960s–1970s, survey expeditions were organized in these northern tropical regions. The researchers discovered that the fawn antechinus was relatively common, although only in locally restricted areas. So our perceptions have changed, while the animal itself has perhaps not.

The smaller, darker, swamp antechinus (*Antechinus minimus*) has a specialized habitat requirement of wet or damp heaths, grassland, or sedgeland. It lives only in Tasmania and along the

Jean-Paul Ferrero/Ardea

RARE AND COMMON

Ravenshoe area

QUEENSLAND

The Atherton antechinus, or Godman's marsupial mouse (*Antechinus godmani*), has one of the most restricted ranges of any marsupial, and possibly of any Australian mammal.

It inhabits less than 385 sq miles (1,000 sq km) of dense forest where the Walter Hill and Cardwell ranges meet near Ravenshoe in northeastern Queensland. The hilly area is about 3,950 ft (1,200 m) above sea level and has an average rainfall of nearly 80 in (200 cm) yearly. Should the habitat become disturbed for any reason, this antechinus would be unlikely to survive.

Such specialized, restricted conditions would put any animal at risk. In fact, the Atherton antechinus is so rarely seen, it was only recognized officially by science as late as the 1920s, being often confused with the similar-looking, but far more common and widespread, yellow-footed antechinus (*Antechinus flavipes*).

The yellow-footed species is the most common mainland antechinus, living all along the eastern side of the continent and in the southwest corner of Western Australia. It has a much wider habitat tolerance and can live in a variety of places from tropical forest to

CONSERVATION MEASURES

To maintain current populations of dasyures, several linked aims are being successfully implemented:

• Increasing public awareness of the dasyures as part of Australia's unique national heritage. As a result, state and national parks, ecologically managed preserves, and sanctuaries have blossomed over the past 20–30 years.

• Further scientific surveys and studies. So much about the marsupial carnivores is still unknown— even the basic distribution of elusive species such as the long-tailed and sandhill dunnarts.

• Local control of introduced competitor and pest species such as feral cats, foxes and rats.

swamps and dry mulga shrubland. In some areas it is familiar in parks, gardens, and homes, where it is a valuable killer of house mice.

But this antechinus's "cheeky" opportunist nature can make it a pest. It moves with great speed and has been known to run upside down across kitchen ceilings in its search for food, making it difficult to catch even for the house cat.

THE YELLOW-FOOTED ANTECHINUS MAY BE A RESOURCEFUL SURVIVOR, BUT ITS TENDENCY TO EXPLOIT MANKIND CAN BRING IT INTO DISFAVOR WITH ITS OFTEN-UNWILLING HUMAN HOSTS.

• Sanctuaries that can be fenced to keep out these intruders and allow the native wildlife to settle.

• Specific "target" preserves for species with extremely limited ranges, such as the dibbler, numbat, sandstone, and Atherton and swamp antechinuses, and the red-tailed phascogale. Preserve management will enable the preservation of suitable vegetation and prey species.

• Captive breeding of the most endangered species for eventual reintroduction to the wild.

DEVILS IN DANGER

THE *RED DATA BOOK* OF THREATENED SPECIES CONTAINS TEN DASYURES:

NUMBAT	ENDANGERED
KOWARI	ENDANGERED
MULGARA	VULNERABLE
NATIVE CAT	ENDANGERED
DIBBLER	ENDANGERED
WAMEENGER	ENDANGERED
KANGAROO ISLAND DUNNART	RARE
CARPENTARIAN DUNNART	RARE
SANDHILL DUNNART	VULNERABLE
JULIA CREEK DUNNART	ENDANGERED

coasts across the Bass Strait, in nearby South Australia, and Victoria. Surveys in the 1970s–1980s discovered previously unrecorded populations, such as those at Carpenter's Rocks in southern Australia and Casterton, Victoria. But the swamp antechinus's "swamps" have also been reduced by human activities, for example at Selbourne and Lake Pedder in Tasmania. The disturbances include mining and other industrial operations, grazing by livestock, and coastal developments such as ports, refineries, and tourist beaches.

FIGHTING BACK

There are many similar tales for other marsupial carnivores. Some, like the dibbler and numbat, have had conservation areas set aside for them. Others are left to fend for themselves, facing competition and predation from introduced species and habitat loss and pollution in various forms. Ten species are now listed in the IUCN's *Red Data Book* of threatened animals.

In recent years there have been some imaginative attempts at redressing the balance. The Australian government has allocated sums in excess of A$1 million to help control cats, foxes, goats, and other introduced species. One controversial possibility is a genetically engineered virus that affects foxes by sterilizing them. Another project involves setting apart large areas surrounded by electric fences, which are then cleared of introduced species, to allow the native wildlife to thrive. The first of such sanctuaries opened in 1982 at

2157

ALONGSIDE MAN

A DEVIL OF A PET

Various people have kept devils in captivity and tried to tame them as domestic pets. Surprisingly, in spite of their fierce reputation, these animals make placid and even friendly companions. Scientists who have trapped and studied wild devils note that they often show little fear at being captured and even allow themselves to be handled. This is in marked contrast to most other marsupial carnivores, which attempt to escape or at least bite back—sometimes with great ferocity, and especially if they have been separated from their kill.

One zookeeper who bred Tasmanian devils called them "delightful and affectionate." A farmer who had two tame devils took them for walks on leashes, like dogs. The unusual pets spent much time washing and grooming themselves, licking their forepaws and then wiping them over their heads in the manner of cats.

Australian mammals (see page 2144). It is about 4.5–6 in (12–15 cm) long with a coat of long, silky, golden-yellow fur. With its shielded snout and massive foreclaws, it is ideally formed for its subterranean lifestyle. It has a stubby little tail (a longer tail would be a hindrance) and a rear-opening pouch typical of the dasyures. The male's genitals are even recessed into his body for extra streamlining. The marsupial mole shows amazing evolutionary convergence with the unrelated moles of Europe and Asia. This unique creature spends its life tunneling, or, rather, "swimming," through the loose, sandy soils of central and northwest Australia. Its main foods are the larvae and pupae of insects such as ants, beetles, sawflies, and moths, as well as worms and other small soil creatures.

So LITTLE IS KNOWN ABOUT DASYURES THAT CERTAIN SPECIES MAY SUFFER THE FATE OF THE THYLACINE, PROTECTED ONLY IN THE TWILIGHT OF ITS EXISTENCE

Warrawong, in the Adelaide Hills. One embittered conservationist remarked that it is of little use simply designating areas as national parks, since the invaders are already there: "There's very little wildlife left in our national parks: just foxes, cats, rabbits, and goats, and greenies in four-wheel drives."

DEEDS OF DARKNESS
The marsupial mole, *Notoryctes typhlops*, is usually included with the marsupial carnivores and is possibly the most specialized and unmistakable of all

Australian scrubland is cleared for use as farmland, resulting in loss of habitat for many creatures.

It is hard to assess the status of such an out-of-sight creature. The marsupial mole is thought to be common, but it is rarely observed. One clue is the rate at which the curious public supply dead specimens, found by chance, to museums. This rate seems fairly constant, although the species' range may have become smaller since European settlement and predation by foxes is a known threat. Its story is typical of so many dasyures; secretive and nocturnal, often no larger than a mouse, its status may remain a mystery until it is too late to help it. ■

ANT/NHPA

INTO THE FUTURE

Illustration Kim Thompson

The Tasmanian devil is one of the few marsupial carnivores whose future seems relatively safe. Being a carrion feeder and a predator on the weak and sickly, it benefits from animals knocked down by road vehicles and from some domestic livestock. One scientific study called the devil a "carnivorous marsupial successfully adapting to a changing environment," while stressing that it was a difficult animal to study in the wild because of its nocturnal activities, dark coloring, secretive habits, and timidity toward humans.

But what of the other marsupial carnivores? Their futures range across the whole spectrum, from relatively secure to critically endangered. Predicting

PREDICTION

NUMBAT NUMBERS

Captive breeding could enable the reintroduction of numbats to habitats from where they had disappeared. With continued vigilance and habitat protection, especially excluding predators from sanctuaries, numbat numbers may rise again.

what will happen to them is a tricky business with both plus and minus factors coming into play.

One positive aspect for the survival of marsupial carnivores is that most are fierce predators, stocky and strong for their size, and able to hold their own in many situations. However, a shadow has been cast over the success of their survival by cats and foxes, which are now widespread, especially in rural and suburban areas. These introduced animals have adapted to their new prey of Australian small mammals and insects, and many small marsupial carnivores are also falling prey to them, as well as losing their own food resources to the newer inhabitants.

Habitat destruction has taken its toll in the past. But, whereas areas of natural land are still being taken for crops, grazing, and other farming uses, most of the agriculturally useful land across Australia has already been commandeered. The speed of habitat change has therefore been reduced and in some places even reversed.

Persecution by humans continues, but on a much-reduced scale. Australians are aware of their unique wildlife as a national treasure, and many more people are eager to ensure its survival. ■

STATE PROTECTION

The numbat has declined drastically in range and numbers during the past two centuries. Its main range is now a small part of Western Australia, west of Ongerup and South of York. The species is protected by state and national laws, like many marsupial carnivores. Numbats live in nature preserves and state forests. But foxes, wild dogs, and other introduced species can usually gain access and present a large threat. Attempts have been made to breed numbats in captivity, as with other species such as the eastern quoll. A breeding colony of numbats was established at Wanneroo in Western Australia, and the first young were reared successfully in 1985.

NOT SO RARE?

Some of the smaller marsupial carnivores are so elusive, and live in such remote regions, that their numbers may have been underestimated in the past. In other words, they are not as rare as was once believed.

Before 1975, the long-tailed dunnart (Sminthopsis longicauda) was known from only three specimens, described in 1895, 1908, and 1940. Then a female was seen in the Gibson Desert of Western Australia. In 1981 a survey expedition trapped nine long-tailed dunnarts in the Gibson Desert Nature Reserve's Young Range of hills. Their habitat of rocky areas, sparsely vegetated with the characteristic small trees called mulgas (a type of acacia) and spinifex grass, stretched for hundreds of square miles, little touched by European influence. However, this should never leave room for complacency.

Published by Marshall Cavendish Corporation
99 White Plains Road
Tarrytown, New York 10591-9001

© Marshall Cavendish Corporation, 1997
© Marshall Cavendish Ltd, 1994

The material in this series was first published in the English language by Marshall Cavendish Limited, of 119 Wardour Street, London W1V 3TD, England.

All rights reserved. No part of this book may be reproduced or utilized in any form or by any means electronic or mechanical, including photocopying, recording, or by any information storage and retrieval system, without prior written permission from the publisher and the copyright holders.

Library of Congress Cataloging-in-Publication Data

Encyclopedia of mammals.
  p. cm.
  Includes index.
  ISBN 0-7614-0575-5 (set)   ISBN 0-7614-0589-5 (v. 14)

  Summary: Detailed articles cover the history, anatomy, feeding habits, social structure, reproduction, territory,
    and current status of ninety-five mammals around the world.
  1. Mammals—Encyclopedias, Juvenile. [l. Mammals—Encyclopedias.]   I. Marshall Cavendish Corporation.
  QL706.2.E54 1996
  599'.003—dc20   96-17736
                                                                     CIP
                                                                     AC

Printed in Malaysia
Bound in U.S.A.